MAKE IT
Sparkle!

25 dazzling jewelry designs
to make any occasion special

Lindsay Burke
OF FUSION BEADS

INTERWEAVE
interweave.com

CONTENTS

INTRODUCTION

Jewelry has been a passion of mine for as long as I can remember.
I remember always admiring and longing for my mother's jewelry.
I especially loved the pieces that sparkled the most. I have since had
a strong need to wear something sparkly every day.

I began making jewelry at a young age after being taught a few techniques
from an older relative. From then on, I continued to learn and grow my
beading skills. I am always observing others making jewelry, taking beading
classes, reading books, and inspecting jewelry to try to figure out how it
was made. I'm always asking myself, "How can I make that?"

The amazing artists and designers that I have known throughout my life
have been a huge influence on my own jewelry designs and aesthetic. I am
constantly amazed and impressed with the talented people that I know
and am surrounded with on a daily basis. They are always pushing me to
be creative and innovative in my own jewelry designs.

Just as I am constantly being influenced by and learning from others,
I hope that this book will inspire and encourage you to create amazing
pieces of jewelry. Feel free to make these pieces exactly as they are shown
or change them to fit your unique personality. Jewelry is the perfect way
to express your individuality and style, so feel free to play, create, and
inspire.

Each jewelry design in this book is created with sparkle in mind and is
intended to add a dazzling touch to all of your outfits, no matter what the
occasion. Have fun and make it sparkle!

Bejeweled
NECKLACE

Designed by Katie Wall

Adorn your ensemble with this breathtaking bib necklace. It's simple to put together, but everyone will think it took you hours to complete.

MATERIALS

15 fern green 4mm crystal bicones (A)

15 fern green 6mm crystal bicones (B)

15 fuchsia 8mm crystal rounds (C)

15 indicolite 12 x 8mm crystal drop minis (D)

1 gunmetal-plated 12 x 7mm lobster-claw clasp

18" (45.5 cm) of gunmetal 3.4mm rolo chain

2 gunmetal 6mm open jump rings 20ga

15 gunmetal 2" (5 cm) eye pins 21ga

30 gunmetal 2" (5 cm) head pins 21ga

Shown here:

(A): 5328 4mm Fern Green Swarovski Crystal Bicone Bead

(B): 5328 6mm Fern Green Swarovski Crystal Bicone Bead

(C): 5000 8mm Fuchsia Swarovski Crystal Round Bead

(D): 5056 12 x 8mm indicolite Swarovski Crystal Drop Mini Bead

TOOLS

Round-nose pliers

Chain-nose pliers

Wire cutters

TECHNIQUES

Simple Loop (page 121)

Opening and Closing a Jump Ring (page 125)

FINISHED LENGTH

20.5" (52 cm)

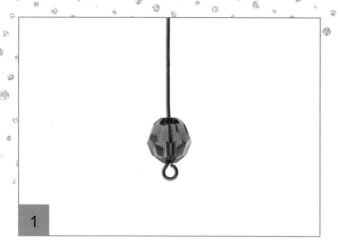

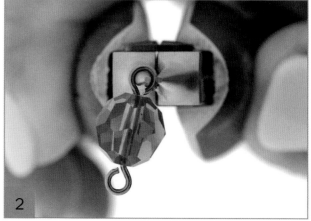

1   Place 1C on an eye pin.

2   Make a simple loop with the remaining wire. This will create one fuchsia unit.

3   Repeat Steps 1–2 for each C. Set all 15 units aside.

4   Place 1D on a head pin. Make a simple loop with the remaining wire. This will create one indicolite unit.

5

5 Repeat Step 4 for each D. Set all 15 units aside.

6

6 Place 1A on a head pin. String the head pin through the center link of the 18" (45.5 cm) length of chain. Place 1B on the head pin.

7

7 Make a simple loop with the remaining wire.

8

8 Repeat Steps 6–7, adding units to every other link of chain on each side of the center link. Work until you have a total of 15 units attached to the chain.

9 Open one of the simple loops of a fuchsia unit from Step 3. Attach it to one simple loop from Step 8. Close the loop.

10 Repeat Step 9 for all 15 units.

11 Open one of the simple loops of one indicolite unit. Attach it to one simple loop of the fuchsia units in Step 10. Close the loop.

12 Repeat Step 11 for all 15 units.

13 Finish the necklace by opening a jump ring and adding it to one end of the chain. Close the jump ring.

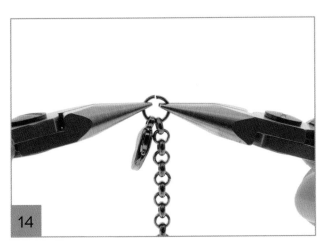

14 Open another jump ring and add it to the other end of the chain. Attach the lobster-claw clasp. Close the jump ring.

Frost Flower

NECKLACE

Crystals form an icy flower pattern in this awe-inspiring bib necklace. This is a jaw-dropping design that can be worn with either a low-cut or a high-cut neckline.

MATERIALS

53 crystal AB 10.5 x 7mm crystal olive beads

14" of sterling silver 4.1mm screw-wire cable chain

23 sterling silver–plated 6mm textured open jump rings 16ga

1 silver-filled 1½" (3.8 cm) head pin 22ga

52 silver-filled 1½" (3.8 cm) eye pins 22ga

1 sterling silver 13.5 x 6.5mm balloon lobster-claw clasp

Shown here:

10.5 x 7mm Crystal AB Preciosa Czech Crystal Olive Bead

6mm Sterling Silver Plated Brass 16-gauge Textured Open Jump Ring by Nunn Design

TOOLS

Round-nose pliers

Chain-nose pliers

Wire cutters

TECHNIQUES

Simple Loop (page 121)

Opening and Closing a Jump Ring (page 125)

FINISHED LENGTH

19" (48.5 cm)

1 Place one crystal olive bead on an eye pin.

2 Create a simple loop with the remaining wire. This will create one unit.

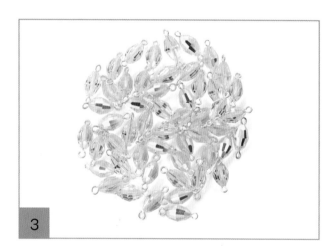

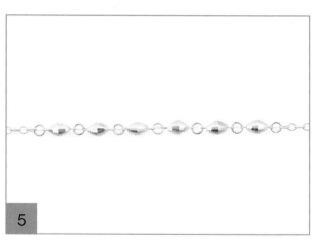

3 Repeat Steps 1–2 to create 52 complete units.

4 Cut the chain into two 7" (18 cm) lengths. Open one textured jump ring. Attach one unit from Step 3 and one 7" (18 cm) length of chain. Close the jump ring.

5 Open a textured jump ring. Attach the unit made in Step 4 and one more unit. Close the jump ring. Repeat until you have 6 units connected to jump rings. Add a jump ring and the other 7" length of chain.

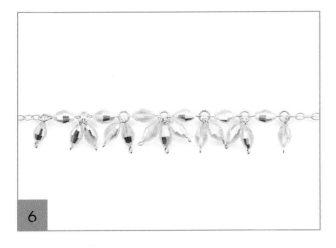

6 Attach the following units to the seven jump rings from Step 5 in the following order:

1st jump ring—attach 1 unit

2nd jump ring—attach 2 units

3rd jump ring—attach 2 units

4th jump ring—attach 3 units

5th jump ring—attach 2 units

6th jump ring—attach 2 units

7th jump ring—attach 1 unit

7 Open a textured jump ring and connect the first two units from Step 6 and add one more unit. Close the jump ring.

Open a textured jump ring and connect the unit added, the next two units from Step 6, and one more unit. Close the jump ring.

Continue adding jump rings and units as shown in the image.

8 Attach the following units to the seven jump rings from Step 7 in the following order:

1st jump ring—attach 1 unit

2nd jump ring—attach 2 units

3rd jump ring—attach 2 units

4th jump ring—attach 3 units

5th jump ring—attach 2 units

6th jump ring—attach 2 units

7th jump ring—attach 1 unit

9 Open a textured jump ring and connect the first two units from Step 8 and add one more unit. Close the jump ring.

Open a textured jump ring and connect the unit added, the next two units from Step 8, and one more unit. Close the jump ring.

Continue adding jump rings and units as shown in the image.

10 Place one olive crystal on a head pin. Create a simple loop. This is one dangle unit.

11 Attach the following units to the five center jump rings from Step 9 in the following order:

1st jump ring—attach 1 unit

2nd jump ring—attach 2 units

3rd jump ring—attach 1 unit, 1 dangle unit from Step 10, and 1 unit

4th jump ring—attach 2 units

5th jump ring—attach 1 unit

12 Attach the bottom units from Step 11 together in sets of two, leaving the center unit free.

13 Finish the necklace by attaching a textured jump ring to the end of one of the lengths of chain.

14 Attach a clasp to the end of the other length of chain with a textured jump ring.

Blue Persuasion
BRACELET

Once you make this cool blue bracelet, there will be no persuading you not to wear it. You're gonna see the light . . . it's so easy.

MATERIALS

7 light turquoise 10mm crystal rounds

7 rhodium-plated pewter 9mm hammered circle rings

2 silver-plated 6 x 4mm open oval jump rings 20ga

1 silver-plated 16 x 12mm pewter toggle clasp

2.5' (76 cm) of silver craft wire 24ga

Shown here:

5000 10mm Light Turquoise Swarovski Crystal Round Bead

9mm Rhodium-Plated Pewter Small Hammered Circle Ring by TierraCast®

16 x 12mm Silver-Plated Pewter Toggle Clasp by TierraCast®

TOOLS

Round-nose Pliers

Chain-nose Pliers

Wire cutters

TECHNIQUES

Wire-Wrapped Link (page 123)

Opening and Closing a Jump Ring (Page 125)

FINISHED LENGTH

7 ½" (19 cm)

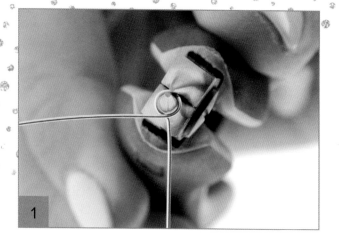

1 Using a 4" (10 cm) piece of wire, begin making a wire-wrapped link.

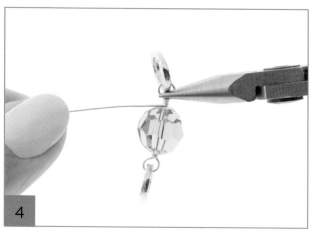

2 Link the loop created in Step 1 into a hammered circle ring. Wrap and cut the excess wire.

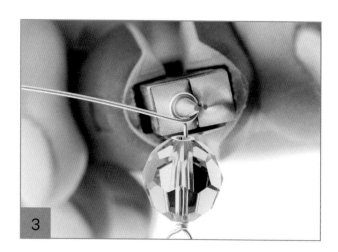

3 Place 1 bead onto the remaining wire. Create a wire-wrapped loop.

4 Link the loop created in Step 3 into a hammered circle ring. Wrap and cut the excess wire.

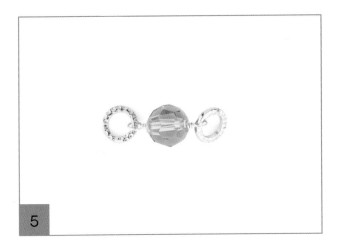

5 Create another wire-wrapped link with 1 bead. Attach it to the hammered circle ring created in Step 4. Wrap and cut the excess wire.

6 Continue linking crystals and hammered circle rings until you have linked 6 crystals and 7 hammered circle rings.

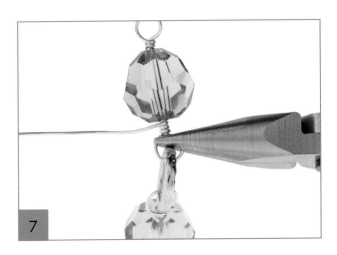

7 Create another wire-wrapped link with 1 bead. Link 1 loop of the link to the last hammered circle ring.

8 Open a jump ring. Attach the bar end of the toggle bar to the remaining loop of the link in Step 7. Close the jump ring.

9 Open a jump ring. Attach the loop end of the toggle bar to the other end of the bracelet. Close the jump ring.

Dazzling
EARRINGS

Designed by Cody Westfall

A dazzling cascade of green crystals and pearls form at the bottom of a drop bead turned upside down. They are delicate earrings that make a big impact.

MATERIALS

2 chrysolite 3mm bicones (A)

2 erinite 3mm bicones (B)

2 chrysolite opal 3mm bicones (C)

2 crystal metallic light gold 2X 3mm bicones (D)

2 crystal iridescent green 3mm bicones (E)

2 iridescent green 3mm pearls (F)

2 chrysolite 4mm bicones (G)

2 erinite 4mm bicones (H)

2 chrysolite opal 4mm bicones (I)

2 Pacific opal 4mm bicones (J)

2 crystal metallic light gold 2X 4mm bicones (K)

2 crystal iridescent green 4mm bicones (L)

2 iridescent green pearl 4mm pearls (M)

2 crystal iridescent green 12 x 8mm crystal drop mini beads (N)

1 pair sterling silver 21mm french hoops with 2mm bead

1" (2.5 cm) of silver-plated 2.8mm curb chain

2 silver-filled 1½" (3.8 cm) eye pins 22ga

26 silver-filled 1½" (3.8 cm) head pins 26ga

Shown here:

(A): 5328 3mm Chrysolite Swarovski Crystal Bicone Bead

(B): 5328 3mm Erinite Swarovski Crystal Bicone Bead

(C): 5328 3mm Chrysolite Opal Swarovski Crystal Bicone Bead

(D): 5328 3mm Crystal Metallic Light Gold 2X Swarovski Bicone Bead

(E): 5328 3mm Crystal Iridescent Green Swarovski Crystal Bicone Bead

(F): 5810 3mm Iridescent Green Swarovski Crystal Pearl

(G): 5328 4mm Chrysolite Swarovski Crystal Bicone Bead

(H): 5328 4mm Erinite Swarovski Crystal Bicone Bead

(I): 5328 4mm Chrysolite Opal Swarovski Crystal Bicone Bead

(J): 5328 4mm Pacific Opal Swarovski Crystal Bicone Bead

(K): 5328 4mm Crystal Metallic Light Gold 2X Swarovski Bicone Bead

(L): 5328 4mm Crystal Iridescent Green Swarovski Crystal Bicone Bead

(M): 5810 4mm Iridescent Green Swarovski Crystal Pearl

(N): 5056 12 x 8mm Crystal Iridescent Green Swarovski Crystal Drop Mini Bead

TOOLS

Round-nose pliers

Chain-nose pliers

Wire cutters

TECHNIQUES

Simple Loop (page 121)

Wire-Wrapped Loop (page 122)

FINISHED LENGTH

2" (5 cm)

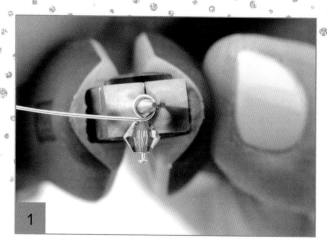

1 Place one 4mm bicone onto a head pin. Begin making a wire-wrapped loop with the head pin. Do not wrap the head pin. Set aside.

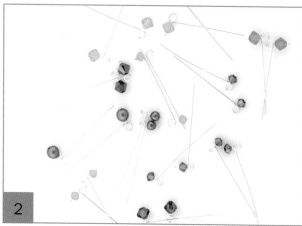

2 Repeat Step 1 for all of the 3mm and 4mm beads.

3 Place 1N onto an eye pin.

4 Turn a simple loop on the other side of the bead.

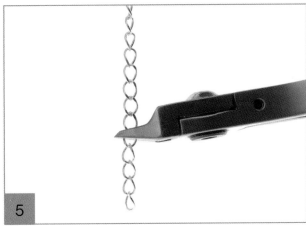

5 Cut two pieces of ½" (1.3 cm) of chain. Make sure you have four links of chain.

6 Attach one loop of the N unit from Step 4 to one piece of chain.

7 Begin attaching the head pins to the chain. Working from the top link of chain, add the beads in the following order:

Left side:	Right side:
1D	1A
1J	1M

Wrap the wire and cut off the remaining wire.

8 Attach and wrap the following beads into the second link of chain in the following order:

Left side:	Right side:
1C	1E
1K	1H

Wrap the wire and cut off the remaining wire.

9 Attach and wrap the following beads into the third link of chain in the following order:

Left side:	Right side:
1F	1B
1G	1I

Wrap the wire and cut off the remaining wire.

10 Attach and wrap 1L to the fourth link of chain.

11 Attach the ear wire to the second simple loop from Step 4. Repeat Steps 1–11 for the second earring.

Pink Party
BRACELETS

Designed by Samantha Slater

Wrap. Stack. Party! Covering basic bangle bracelets with rhinestone chain and crystals will take the boring and make it extraordinary. Start with one and keep adding to your collection.

MATERIALS

62 rose 4mm crystal bicones (A)

62 pink sapphire 4mm crystal bicones (B)

62 Indian pink 4mm crystal bicones (C)

8½" (21.5 cm) of fuchsia 3mm silver-plated crystal rhinestone chain

8½" (21.5 cm) of light Siam 3mm silver-plated crystal rhinestone chain

5 antiqued silver 8½" (21.5 cm) large flat bangle bracelets

30' (9 m) of silver craft wire 26ga

Hypo Tube Cement

Shown here:

(A): 4mm Rose Preciosa Czech Crystal Bicone Bead

(B): 4mm Pink Sapphire Preciosa Czech Crystal Bicone Bead

(C): 4mm Indian Pink Preciosa Czech Crystal Bicone Bead

8½" (21.5 cm) Antique Silver-Plated Brass Large Flat Bangle Bracelet by Nunn Design

TOOLS

Chain-nose pliers

Wire cutters

TECHNIQUES

Covering a Component (page 124)

FINISHED LENGTH

8½" (21.5 cm)

MAKE THE BICONE-COVERED BANGLE.

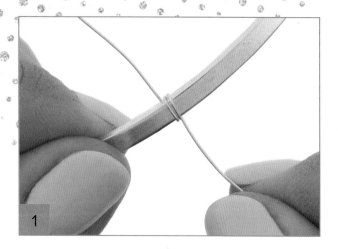

1   Use 6' (1.8 m) of wire to anchor the beads to the bangle. Begin by holding the bangle and an inch of the wire in one hand. Then, with your other hand, lay the wire over the top of the bangle. Wrap the wire around the bangle 2–3 times.

2   Add 1C to the wire. Rest the bicone bead on top of the bangle. Wrap the wire around the bangle once to secure the bicone in place.

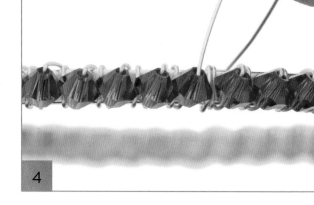

3   Add another C to the wire. Rest the bicone bead on top of the bangle. Wrap the wire around the bangle once to secure the bicone in place.

4   Repeat Step 3 until the bangle is completely covered.

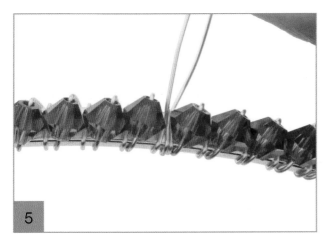

5 To finish off the wire, wrap the wire once or twice around the bangle between the bicone beads.

6 Cut off the excess wire.

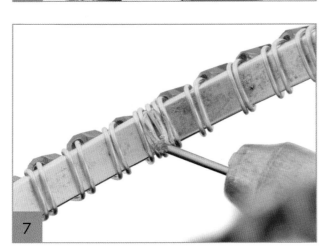

7 Add a drop of glue to the cut ends of the wire. Let dry completely before wearing. Repeat Steps 1–7 for the pink sapphire 4mm crystal bicones and the rose 4mm crystal bicones.

MAKE THE RHINESTONE-CHAIN-COVERED BANGLE.

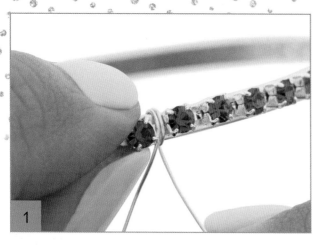

1 Use an 8½" (21.5 cm) piece of fuchsia 3mm silver-plated crystal rhinestone chain. Use 6' (1.8 m) of wire to anchor the chain to the bangle. Begin by holding the bangle and an inch of the wire in one hand. Then, with your other hand, lay the chain over the top of the bangle. Wrap the wire around the bangle three times in between the first two rhinestones.

2 Wrap the wire in between the next two rhinestones three times.

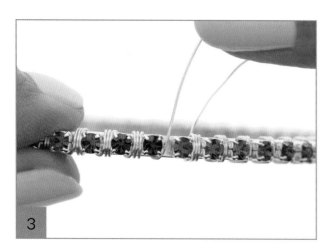

3 Continue wrapping the wire three times in between each rhinestone until the bangle is completely covered.

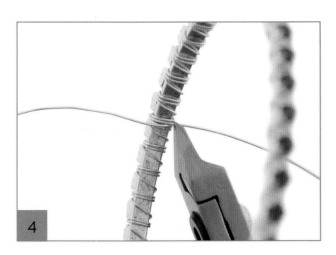

4   To finish off the wire, wrap the wire once between the first and second rhinestones in Step 1. Cut off the excess wire.

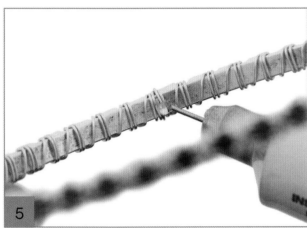

5   Add a drop of glue to the cut ends of the wire. Let dry completely before wearing. Repeat Steps 1–5 for the light Siam 3mm silver-plated crystal rhinestone chain.

Wrapped in Gold

BRACELET

Use memory wire to make a big-impact piece of jewelry with little effort. I made this bracelet so that it is six complete wraps. But you can add more beads if you want more wraps, or you can create a piece with only a few wraps. This is also a great design to use your leftover beads.

MATERIALS

6 g 24k gold-plated metal size 8° seed beads (A)

2 g gold-lined crystal clear hex size 11° seed beads (B)

3 g rosaline amber 4mm tri-bead seed beads (C)

31 crystal golden flare 2X 3mm crystals rounds (D)

21 crystal aurum 4mm crystal bicones (E)

28 crystal celsian 4mm crystal bicones (F)

20 crystal golden flare 2X 3mm crystal bicones (G)

9 crystal celsian 6mm crystal bicones (H)

19 crystal aurum 6mm crystal rounds (I)

6 turns gold-plated memory wire 2¼" (5.5 cm) dia. bracelet

Shown here:

(A): Gold Plated Metal Round Seed Bead

(B): Gold-Lined Crystal Clear Hex Japanese Seed Beads by Toho 989

(C): 4mm Rosaline Amber Tri-Bead Seed Beads

(D): 3mm Crystal Golden Flare 2X Preciosa Czech Crystal Round Bead

(E): 4mm Crystal Aurum Preciosa Czech Crystal Bicone Bead

(F): 4mm Crystal Celsian Preciosa Czech Crystal Bicone Bead

(G): 6mm Crystal Golden Flare 2X Preciosa Czech Crystal Bicone Bead

(H): 6mm Crystal Celsian Preciosa Czech Crystal Bicone Bead

(I): 6mm Crystal Aurum Preciosa Czech Crystal Round Bead

TOOLS

Round-nose pliers

Memory-wire cutters

TECHNIQUES

Simple Loop (page 121)

FINISHED LENGTH

6 turns

TIP

You may need to add or subtract a bead to make the pattern work for you.

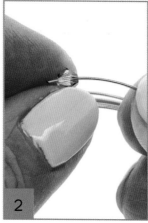

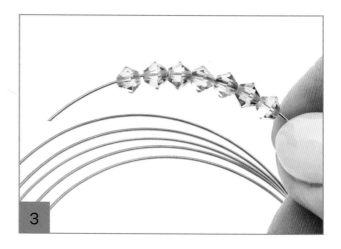

1 Cut your memory wire so that you have about six turns of the wire. Turn a loop on one end of the memory wire. Make sure that the loop is completely closed so that beads don't slide off the wire.

3 Add 2" (5 cm) of crystal celsian 4mm crystal bicones (about 14 bicone beads). Slide all of these beads down the wire to the loop you created in Step 1.

2 String beads on the wire using the end opposite of the loop created in Step 1.

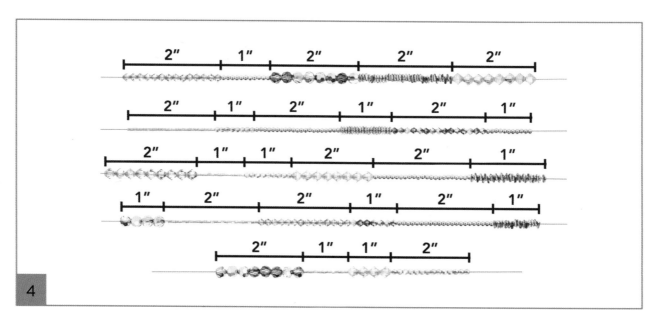

4 Continue adding beads in the following order:

1" (2.5 cm)—24k gold-plated metal size 8° seed beads (about 11 beads) (A)

2" (5 cm)—crystal aurum 6mm crystal rounds (about 8 beads) (I)

2" (5 cm)—rosaline amber 4mm tri-bead seed beads (about 33 beads) (C)

2" (5 cm)—crystal golden flare 2X 6mm crystal bicones (about 8 beads) (G)

2" (5 cm)—gold-lined crystal clear hex size 11° seed beads (about 27 beads) (B)

1" (2.5 cm)—crystal golden flare 2X 3mm crystal rounds (about 8 beads) (D)

2" (5 cm)—24k gold-plated metal size 8° seed beads (about 22 beads) (A)

1" (2.5 cm)—rosaline amber 4mm tri-bead seed beads (about 19 beads) (C)

2" (5 cm)—crystal aurum 4mm crystal bicones (about 14 beads) (E)

1" (2.5 cm)—24k gold-plated metal size 8° seed beads (about 11 beads) (A)

2" (5 cm)—crystal celsian 6mm crystal bicones (about 9 beads) (H)

1" (2.5 cm)—gold-lined crystal clear hex size 11° seed beads (about 14 beads) (B)

1" (2.5 cm)—crystal golden flare 2X 3mm crystal rounds (about 9 beads) (D)

2" (5 cm)—crystal golden flare 2X 6mm crystal bicones (about 8 beads) (G)

2" (5 cm)—24k gold-plated metal size 8° seed beads (about 22 beads) (A)

1" (2.5 cm)—rosaline amber 4mm tri-bead seed beads (about 19 beads) (C)

1" (2.5 cm)—crystal aurum 6mm crystal rounds (about 4 beads) (I)

2" (5 cm)—gold-lined crystal clear hex size 11° seed beads (about 27 beads) (B)

2" (5 cm)—crystal celsian 4mm crystal bicones (about 14 beads) (F)

1" (2.5 cm)—crystal aurum 4mm crystal bicones (about 7 beads) (E)

2" (5 cm)—gold-lined crystal clear hex size 11° seed beads (about 27 beads) (B)

1" (2.5 cm)—rosaline amber 4mm tri-bead seed beads (about 19 beads) (C)

2" (5 cm)—crystal aurum 6mm crystal rounds (about 8 beads) (H)

1" (2.5 cm)—gold-lined crystal clear hex size 11° seed beads (about 14 beads) (B)

1" (2.5 cm)—crystal golden flare 2X 6mm crystal bicones (about 4 beads) (G)

2" (5 cm)—crystal golden flare 2X 3mm crystal rounds (about 14 beads) (D)

5

5 Finish the bracelet when you have about ½" (1.3 cm) of wire left. Use your round-nose pliers to turn a loop with the remaining memory wire. Make sure that the loop is completely closed so that the beads don't slide off the wire.

Tonight's THE Night EARRINGS

Designed by Cody Westfall

Use beading hoops to string metal beads and crystals graduating in size. Tonight will be the night when everyone will be looking at you!

MATERIALS

16 gold-plated 2 x 3mm faceted spacers (A)

8 gold-plated 3mm crystal rhinestone rondelles (B)

8 gold-plated 5mm crystal rhinestone rondelles (C)

4 gold-plated 6mm crystal rhinestone rondelles (D)

4 sterling silver oxidized 2 x 3.5mm corrugated saucer beads (E)

4 sterling silver oxidized 3 x 4.5mm corrugated saucer beads (F)

4 silver-plated 1.5 x 5mm heishi spacer beads (G)

4 crystal 4mm rondelles (H)

12 crystal 6mm rondelles (I)

2 crystal 8mm rondelles (J)

2 sterling silver 4mm open jump rings 20.5ga

2 sterling silver 30mm beading hoops

1 pair sterling silver 21mm french hoops with 2mm bead

Shown here:

(A): 2 x 3mm Gold Plated Pewter Faceted Spacer by TierraCast®

(B): 3mm Crystal Swarovski Crystal Gold-Plated Rhinestone Rondelle

(C): 5mm Crystal Swarovski Crystal Gold-Plated Rhinestone Rondelle

(D): 6mm Crystal Swarovski Crystal Gold Plated Rhinestone Rondelle

(E): 2 x 3.5mm Sterling Silver Oxidized Corrugated Saucer Bead

(F): 3 x 4.5mm Sterling Silver Oxidized Corrugated Saucer Bead

(G): 1.5 x 5mm Silver-Plated Pewter Heishi Spacer Bead by TierraCast®

(H): 5040 4mm Crystal Swarovski Crystal Rondelle Bead

(I): 5040 6mm Crystal Swarovski Crystal Rondelle Bead

(J): 5040 8mm Crystal Swarovski Crystal Rondelle Bead

TOOLS

Round-nose pliers

Chain-nose pliers

Wire cutters

TECHNIQUES

Simple Loop (page 121)

Opening and Closing a Jump Ring (page 125)

FINISHED LENGTH

2" (5 cm)

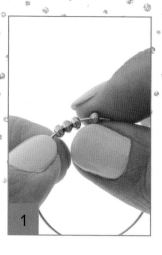 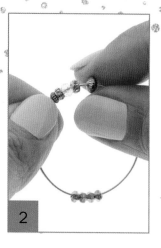  

1   String 4A onto the beading hoop.

2   String beads onto the beading hoop in the following sequence: 1E, 1B, 1H, 1B, 1F.

3   String beads onto the beading hoop in the following sequence: 1C, 1I, 1C, 1I, 1G, 1I.

4   String beads onto the beading hoop in the following sequence: 1D, 1J, 1D.

 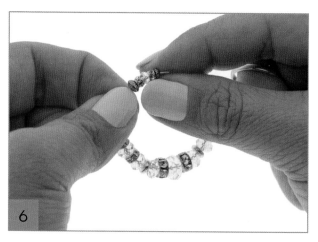

5   String beads onto the beading hoop in the following sequence: 1I, 1G, 1I, 1C, 1I, 1C.

6   String beads onto the beading hoop in the following sequence: 1F, 1B, 1H, 1B, 1E.

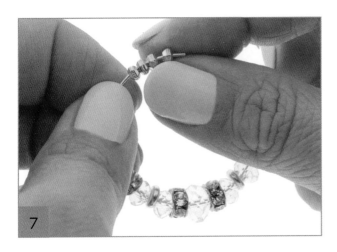

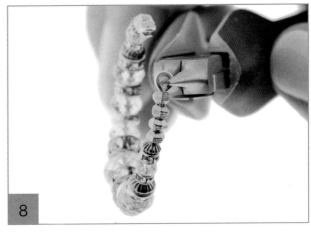

7 String 4A onto the beading hoop.

8 Turn a simple loop on the other end of the beading hoop, making sure to turn the loop so that it is on the same plane as the existing loop.

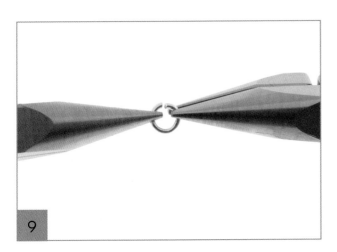

9 Open one jump ring.

10 Attach both loops of the beading hoop and one ear wire. Close the jump ring.

Repeat Steps 1–10 for the second earring.

Yours Truly
NECKLACE

Designed by Cody Westfall

Create a striking silhouette with this dazzling bib necklace. Faceted crystals in a tiered trio of colors are complemented by gunmetal chain.

MATERIALS

52 crystal silver night 4mm crystal rondelle beads (A)

65 crystal metallic light gold 2X 4mm bicone beads (B)

7 crystal rose gold 2X 8mm crystal circle pendants (C)

1 gunmetal-plated 12 x 7mm lobster-claw clasp

20½" (52 cm) of gunmetal-plated 3mm oval link cable chain

6 gunmetal-plated 2" (5 cm) head pins 21ga

20 gunmetal-plated 2" (5 cm) eye pins 21ga

8 gunmetal-plated 4mm open jump rings 21ga

1 gunmetal-plated 6mm open jump ring 20ga

Shown here:

(A): 5040 4mm Crystal Silver Night Swarovski Crystal Rondelle Bead

(B): 5328 4mm Crystal Metallic Light Gold 2X Swarovski Bicone Bead

(C): 6428 8mm Crystal Rose Gold 2X Swarovski Crystal Circle Pendant

TOOLS

Round-nose pliers

Chain-nose pliers

Wire cutters

TECHNIQUES

Simple Loop (page 121)

Opening and Closing a Jump Ring (page 125)

FINISHED LENGTH

18½" (47 cm)

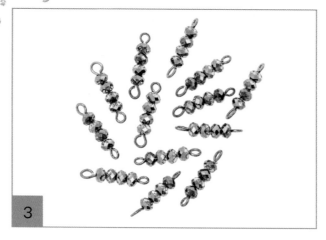

1 String 4A on an eye pin.

2 Make a simple loop with the remaining wire. This will make one rondelle link.

3 Repeat Steps 1–2 for a total of thirteen links. Set aside.

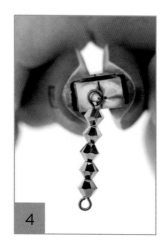

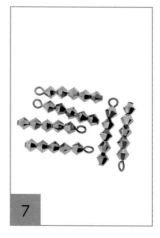

4 String 5B on an eye pin. Make a simple loop with the remaining wire. This will make one bicone link.

5 Repeat Step 4 for a total of seven links. Set aside.

6 String 5B on a head pin. Make a simple loop with the remaining wire. This will make one bicone dangle.

7 Repeat Step 6 for a total of six bicone dangles. Set aside.

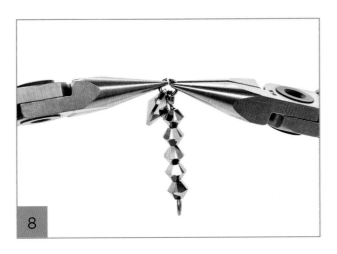

8 Open a 4mm jump ring. Add one bicone link from Step 5 and a round pendant. Close the jump ring.

9 Repeat for each of the seven bicone links.

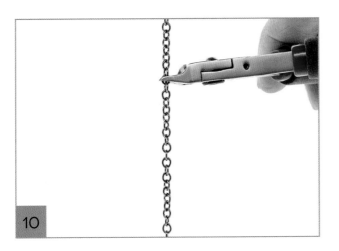

10 Cut the chain into two lengths. One piece of chain should be 2½" (6.5 cm) long (25 links). The second length of chain should be 18" (45.5 cm) long.

11 Find the center link of the 18" (45.5 cm) piece of chain. Open one loop of a rondelle link from Step 3 and add it to the center link of the chain. Close the loop.

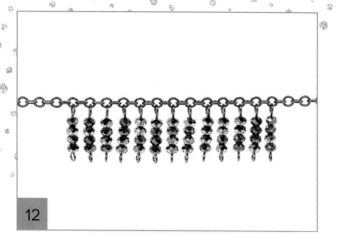

12 Working from the center of the chain out, continue adding a rondelle link to every other chain link. The thirteen links should be centered on the chain.

13 Starting at one end of the smaller piece of chain, attach the opposite end of the rondelle links from Step 12.

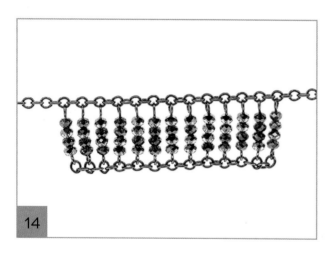

14 Continue attaching each of the rondelle links to every other chain link.

15 Attach one bicone link from Step 9 to the first link of chain.

16 Skip one chain link and attach a bicone dangle from Step 7 to the next chain link.

17 Skip one chain link and attach another bicone link to the next link of chain. Repeat the pattern with the remaining links and dangles.

18 Add a clasp to one side of the chain with a 4mm jump ring.

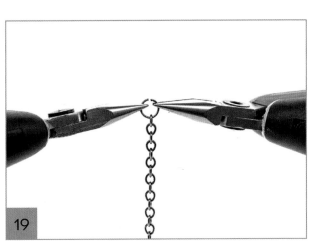

19 Add a 6mm jump ring to the other end of the chain.

Evening Gold
BRACELET

Designed by Allison Hoffmann

An evening of glitter and gold is what every girl wants. Create a perfect match to your ensemble by easily switching the crystals to a matching color. The gold accents complement the brilliant sparkle of the crystals.

MATERIALS

42 crystal AB 4mm crystal bicones

26 crystal AB 6mm crystal rounds

1 gold-plated 16 x 12mm pewter toggle clasp

12" (30.5 cm) of crystal AB 3mm gold-plated crystal rhinestone chain

8 gold-plated 6mm open jump rings 18ga

2 gold-plated 12mm open jump rings 13ga

4 gold-filled crimp beads 2 x 2mm

4 gold-filled crimp bead covers 3.5mm

4 gold-plated 8 x 4mm ends for crystal rhinestone chain

2' (61 cm) of clear beading wire .014 dia.

Shown here:

4mm Crystal AB Preciosa Czech Crystal Bicone Bead

6mm Crystal AB Preciosa Czech Crystal Round Bead

TOOLS

Crimping pliers

Chain-nose pliers

Wire cutters

TECHNIQUES

Crimping (page 120)

Using a Crimp Cover (page 121)

Opening and Closing a Jump Ring (page 125)

FINISHED LENGTH

8" (20.5 cm)

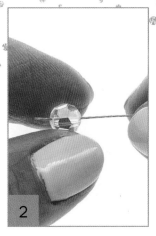

1. Close the two 12mm jump rings. Crimp 1' (30.5 cm) of beading wire to one of the 12mm jump rings.

2. String 26 crystal AB 6mm crystal rounds on the beading wire.

3. Crimp the other end of the beading wire to the second 12mm jump ring.

4. Repeat Steps 2–3 with the remaining 1' (30.5 cm) of beading wire and the 42 crystal AB 4mm crystal bicones.

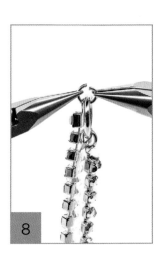

5. Cut two 6" (15 cm) pieces of the rhinestone chain (about 32 crystals each).

6. Set the last stone of the chain in a prong end for the rhinestone chain.

7. Secure the stone in the end by gently folding down the prongs with your chain-nose pliers. Repeat Steps 6–7 for each end of the rhinestone chain.

8. Attach the rhinestone chain to one 12mm jump ring using a 6mm jump ring. Attach the other end of the chain to the opposite 12mm jump ring.

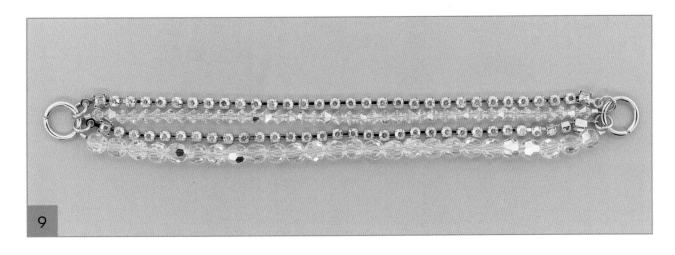

9 Repeat Step 8 for the second piece of rhinestone chain. The rhinestone chain should sit in between the two strands of beads.

10 Attach a clasp to one of the 12mm jump rings using two 6mm jump rings.

11 Attach the other end of the clasp to the other 12mm jump ring using two 6mm jump rings.

12 Finish the bracelet by using crimp covers to cover the four crimp beads.

Raindrops AND Lilies EARRINGS

Just as rain falls and dances off the petals of lilies, so do these crystals in this sweet pair of earrings. The combination will glisten and move with every move you make.

MATERIALS

20 indicolite 3mm crystal bicones (A)

8 indicolite 4mm crystal bicones (B)

10 peridot opal 6 x 9mm day lily pressed-glass beads (C)

18 silver-plated 2" (5 cm) head pins 24ga

3" (7.5 cm) of silver-plated 2mm flat oval link cable chain

1 pair sterling silver 14mm ear wires with 2mm bead

Shown here:

(A): 5328 3mm Indicolite Swarovski Crystal Bicone Bead

(B): 5328 4mm Indicolite Swarovski Crystal Bicone Bead

(C): 6 x 9mm Peridot Opal Day Lily Czech Pressed-Glass Bead

TOOLS

Round-nose pliers

Chain-nose pliers

Wire cutters

TECHNIQUES

Wire-Wrapped Loop (page 122)

FINISHED LENGTH

2½" (6.5 cm)

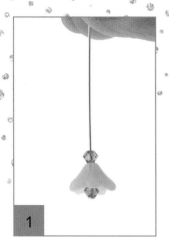

1

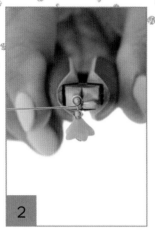

2

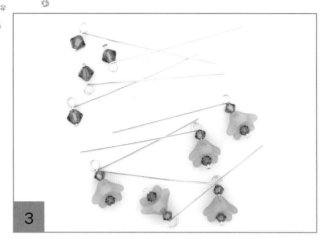

3

1 Place 1A, 1C, and 1A on a head pin. Begin making a wire-wrapped loop but do not wrap it. Set aside.

2 Repeat Step 1 for a total of five lily units. Set aside.

3 Place 1B on a head pin. Begin making a wire-wrapped loop but do not wrap it. Set aside. Repeat for a total of four bicone units.

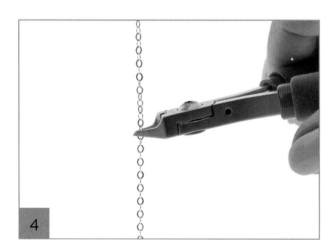

4

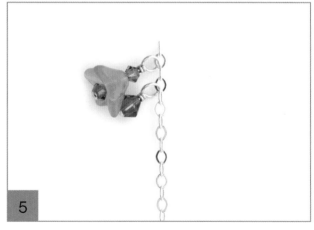

5

4 Cut one 1½" (3.8 cm) piece of chain. The length of chain should be 18 links long.

5 Begin building the earring from the top down. Add one lily unit to the second chain link from the top. Make sure that the dangle hangs on the left side of the chain link. Wrap and cut off the excess wire.

Add one bicone unit to the fourth chain link from the top. Make sure that the dangle hangs on the left side of the chain link. Wrap and cut off the excess wire.

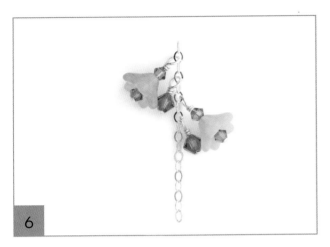

6 Add one lily unit to the sixth chain link from the top. Make sure that the dangle hangs on the right side of the chain link. Wrap and cut the excess wire.

Add one bicone unit to the eighth chain link from the top. Make sure that the dangle hangs on the right side of the chain link. Wrap and cut off the excess wire.

7 Repeat Step 5 for the tenth and twelfth chain links.

8 Repeat Step 6 for the fourteenth and sixteenth chain links.

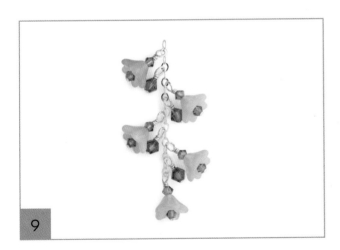

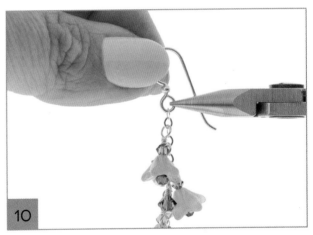

9 Add one lily unit to the last link of the chain. Wrap and cut off the excess wire.

10 Attach the ear wire to the first link of the chain.

Repeat Steps 1–10 for the remaining earring.

Stack Them Up
BRACELETS

Designed by Cody Westfall

Bangles embellished with Swarovski crystal beads stack easily for some serious arm candy. Play with color to match all of your favorite ensembles.

MATERIALS

6 crystal paradise shine 14 x 9.5mm emerald-cut beads

3 amethyst 14 x 9.5mm emerald-cut beads

3 sterling silver–plated $8\frac{1}{2}$" (21.5cm) large flat bangle bracelets

22.5' (7m) of silver craft wire 26ga

Hypo Tube Cement

Shown here:

5515 14 x 9.5mm Crystal Paradise Shine Swarovski Crystal Emerald-Cut Beads

5515 14 x 9.5mm Amethyst Swarovski Crystal Emerald-Cut Beads

$8\frac{1}{2}$" (21.5cm) Sterling Silver Plated Brass Large Flat Bangle Bracelet by Nunn Design

TOOLS

Wire cutters

Chain-nose pliers

TECHNIQUES

Covering a Component (page 124)

FINISHED LENGTH

$8\frac{1}{2}$" (21.5 cm)

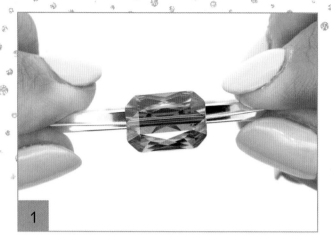

1 Cut a 2.5′ (76cm) piece of wire. Add one emerald-cut bead to the center of the wire. Lay it on the edge of the bangle.

2 Wrap one side of the wire around the bangle 2–3 times to anchor it.

3 Repeat Step 2 for the other side of the wire.

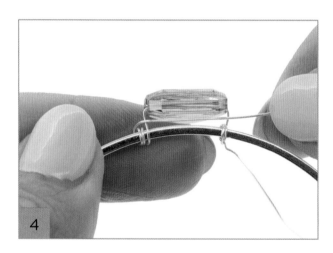

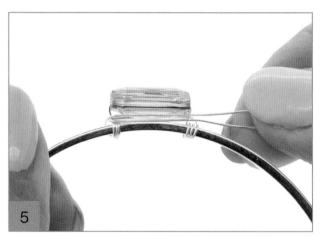

4 To stabilize the bead on the bangle, begin wrapping one end of the wire at the base of the bead.

5 Once you have wrapped the wire 1–2 times, wrap the second piece of wire around the base of the bead.

6 Continue wrapping both pieces of wire around the base of the wire. The wire should be wrapped organically to create a messy look.

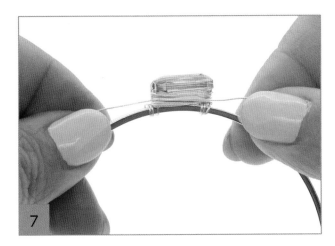

7

8

9

7 When you have wrapped the base of the bead several times, split the two pieces of wire so there is one on each side of the bead.

8 Secure the ends of the wire by wrapping the ends around the bangle 2–3 times.

9 Cut off the excess wire.

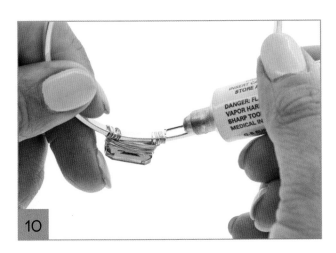

10

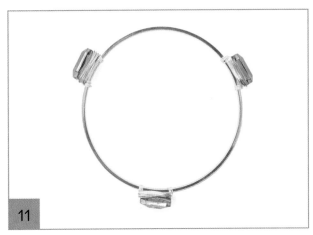

11

10 Add a drop of glue to the ends of the wire and let dry completely.

11 Add two more beads to the bangle by repeating Steps 1–10.

Repeat Steps 1–11 for the remaining two bangles.

Tiger Lily

EARRINGS

Bursting with bold colors, these easy earrings will be the pop of color you need. A beaded ring adds an extra touch of style.

MATERIALS

2 fuchsia 8mm crystal rounds

2 tangerine 13mm crystal pendants

2 antiqued silver-plated pewter 12mm beaded circle rings

1 pair sterling silver 14mm ear wires with 2mm bead

2 silver-plated 6mm open jump rings 20ga

2 silver-plated 2" (5 cm) eye pins 21ga

Shown here:

5000 8mm Fuchsia Swarovski Crystal Round Bead

6010 13mm Tangerine Swarovski Crystal Pendant

TOOLS

Round-nose pliers

Chain-nose pliers

Wire cutters

TECHNIQUES

Simple Loop (page 121)

Opening and Closing a Jump Ring (page 125)

FINISHED LENGTH

2" (5 cm)

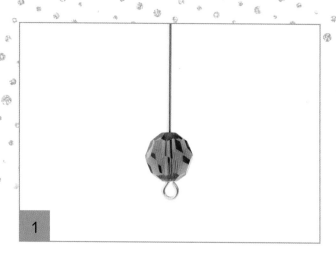

1 Place one fuchsia crystal round bead on an eye pin.

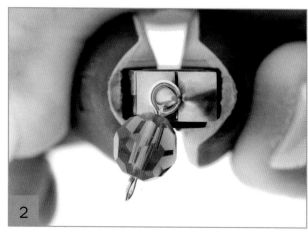

2 Create a simple loop with the remaining wire. This will create one round-link unit.

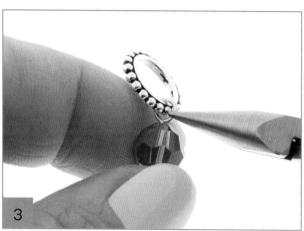

3 Open one loop of the link created in Step 2. Attach the loop to a beaded circle ring. Close the loop.

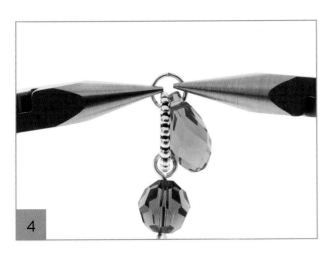

4 Open one 6mm jump ring. Attach one tangerine crystal pendant and the beaded circle ring from Step 3. Close the jump ring.

5 Attach an ear wire to the second loop of the link created in Step 2.

Repeat Steps 1–5 for the second earring.

Rain City
EARRINGS

Drops of Swarovski crystal drip from silver teardrop components. You'll be dancing in the rain with these earrings!

MATERIALS

2 crystal paradise shine 16mm crystal pear-shaped pendants

2 crystal paradise shine 22mm crystal pear-shaped pendants

2 sterling silver 40 x 28 flat teardrop components

1 pair silver-filled 20.5mm french hoops

2 sterling silver 3.5mm open jump rings 22ga

4 sterling silver 6mm open jump rings 20.5ga

Shown here:

6106 16mm Crystal Paradise Shine Swarovski Crystal Pear-Shaped Pendant

6106 22mm Crystal Paradise Shine Swarovski Crystal Pear-Shaped Pendant

TOOLS

Chain-nose pliers

TECHNIQUES

Opening and Closing a Jump Ring (page 125)

FINISHED LENGTH

2 ³⁄₄" (7 cm)

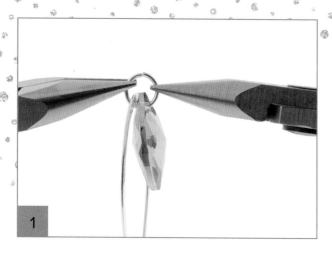

1 Open a 6mm jump ring. Attach a 16mm pendant.

2 Make sure that the crystal is at the bottom of the component.

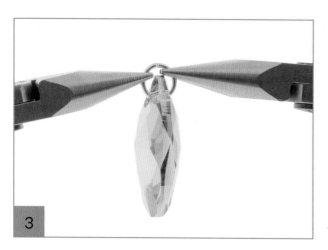

3 Open a 6mm jump ring. Attach it to the 22mm pendant. Close the jump ring.

4 Open a 3.5mm jump ring. Attach it to the jump ring in Step 3. Close the jump ring.

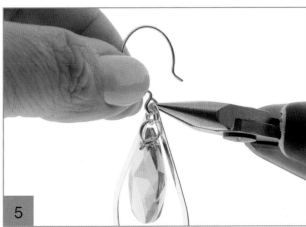

5 Open the loop of the ear wire. Attach the jump ring from Step 4 and the teardrop component from Step 2. Close the loop of the ear wire.

Repeat Steps 1–5 for the second earring.

Watermelon
BRACELET

This charm bracelet is bursting with delicious color. Create a unique bracelet that you can continue adding special charms to.

MATERIALS

1 fern green 7.1mm crystal xirius flat-back rhinestone

1 fuchsia crystal silver-plated 10 x 5mm navette channel charm

1 crystal vitrail medium 14mm crystal Greek cross pendant

1 antiqued silver-plated 13.5 x 10.5mm glue-in plain bezel charm

1 sterling silver-plated 17 x 14mm small disk charm with crystal

3 silver-plated 6mm open jump rings 18ga

1 silver-plated 7mm open jump ring 18ga

1 bright silver expandable charm bangle bracelet

E6000 adhesive 0.18 oz tube

Shown here:

2088 SS34 Fern Green Swarovski Crystal Xirius Flat-Back Rhinestone

10 x 5mm Fuchsia Swarovski Crystal Silver-Plated Navette Channel Charm

6867 14mm Crystal Vitrail Medium Swarovski Crystal Greek Cross Pendant

13.5 x 10.5mm Antiqued Silver-Plated Pewter SS34 Glue in Plain Bezel Charm by TierraCast®

17 x 14mm Sterling Silver-Plated Pewter Small Disk Charm with Crystal by Nunn Design

17 x 14mm Sterling Silver-Plated Pewter Small Disk Charm with Crystal by Nunn Design

TOOLS

Chain-nose pliers

TECHNIQUES

Opening and Closing a Jump Ring (page 125)

1 Add a small drop of glue to the bezel charm using a toothpick.

2 Place the flat-back crystal rhinestone in the bezel charm.

3 Gently press the flat back so that it is set in the bezel. Let dry completely.

4 Use a 6mm jump ring to add the bezel charm from Step 3 to the bangle. Close the jump ring.

5 Use a 6mm jump ring to add the fuchsia navette channel charm to the bangle. Close the jump ring.

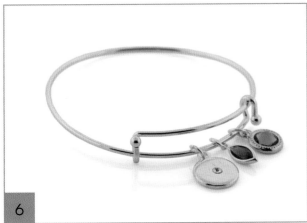

6 Use a 6mm jump ring to add the disk charm to the bangle. Close the jump ring.

7 Use a 7mm jump ring to add the crystal cross pendant to the bangle. Close the jump ring.

Dance *till Dawn*

EARRINGS

You will be dancing until the sun comes up in these breathtaking cluster earrings.

MATERIALS

12 amethyst 6mm crystal bicones (A)

4 amethyst 5mm crystal bicones (B)

8 fuchsia 5mm crystal bicones (C)

4 fuchsia 4mm crystal bicones (D)

8 tangerine 4mm crystal bicones (E)

4 tangerine 3mm crystal bicones (F)

10 sunflower 3mm crystal bicones (G)

3" (7.5 cm) of sterling silver 2.6mm flat cable chain

1 pair sterling silver 14mm ear wires

50 sterling silver 2" (5 cm) head pins 26ga

Shown here:

(A): 5328 6mm Amethyst Swarovski Crystal Bicone Bead

(B): 5328 5mm Amethyst Swarovski Crystal Bicone Bead

(C): 5328 5mm Fuchsia Swarovski Crystal Bicone Bead

(D): 5328 4mm Fuchsia Swarovski Crystal Bicone Bead

(E): 5328 4mm Tangerine Swarovski Crystal Bicone Bead

(F): 5328 3mm Tangerine Swarovski Crystal Bicone Bead

(G): 5328 3mm Sunflower Swarovski Crystal Bicone Bead

TOOLS

Round-nose pliers

Chain-nose pliers

Wire cutters

TECHNIQUES

Wire-Wrapped Loop (page 122)

FINISHED LENGTH

$2\frac{1}{4}$" (5.5 cm)

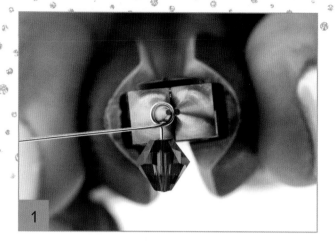

1

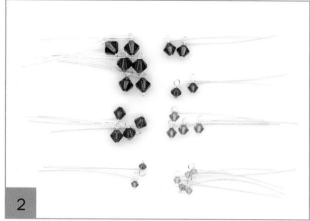

2

1 Place 1A on a head pin. Begin making a wire-wrapped loop but do not wrap it.

2 Repeat Step 1 for all of the remaining bicones. You will have the following looped dangle units for one earring:

6A	2D	5G
2B	4E	
4C	2F	

Set aside.

3

4

5

6

3 Cut a 1½" (3.8 cm) piece of chain. The length of chain should be 13 links long.

4 Begin building the earring from the top down. Add two A dangle units to each of the top three chain links. One dangle should be on each side of the chain link. Wrap the wire and cut off the excess wire.

5 Add two B dangle units to the fourth chain link. Make sure that there is one unit on each side of the link.

6 Add two C units to the fifth and sixth chain links. Make sure that there is one unit on each side of the links.

7 Add two D dangle units to the seventh chain link. Make sure that there is one unit on each side of the link.

8 Add two D dangle units to the eighth and ninth chain links. Make sure that there is one unit on each side of the links.

9 Add two E dangle units to the tenth chain link. Make sure that there is one unit on each side of the link.

10 Add two F dangle units to the eleventh and twelfth chain links. Make sure that there is one unit on each side of the links. And add one F dangle unit to the thirteenth chain link.

11 Attach an ear wire to the first link of chain from Step 4.

Repeat for the second earring.

Party
ON MY *Wrist*
BRACELET

Designed by Katie Wall

Fun, bright colors dance playfully in this bracelet. Link larger beads together with jump rings and then add movement by dangling crystal bicones from the jump rings. You can easily change the colors you use to work with your outfit.

MATERIALS

5 fuchsia 4mm crystal bicones (A)

3 blue zircon 4mm crystal bicones (B)

4 amethyst 4mm crystal bicones (C)

4 indicolite 4mm crystal bicones (D)

3 fern green 4mm crystal bicones (E)

3 denim blue 4mm crystal bicones (F)

1 fern green 8mm crystal round mini bead (G)

1 fern green 8mm crystal square mini bead (H)

1 fern green 10 x 8mm crystal oval mini bead (I)

1 indicolite 8mm crystal round mini bead (K)

1 indicolite 8mm crystal square mini bead (L)

1 indicolite 10 x 8mm crystal oval mini bead (M)

1 amethyst 8mm crystal round mini bead (N)

1 amethyst 10 x 8mm crystal oval mini bead (O)

1 gold-plated 9.5 x 5.5mm lobster-claw clasp

21 gold-plated 1½" (3.8 cm) head pins 21ga

9 gold-plated 6mm open jump rings 21ga

18" (45.5 cm) of gold color round wire 22ga

Shown here:

(A): 5328 4mm Fuchsia Swarovski Crystal Bicone Bead

(B): 5328 4mm Blue Zircon Swarovski Crystal Bicone Bead

(C): 5328 4mm Amethyst Swarovski Crystal Bicone Bead

(D): 5328 4mm Indicolite Swarovski Crystal Bicone Bead

(E): 5328 4mm Fern Green Swarovski Crystal Bicone Bead

(F): 5328 4mm Denim Blue Swarovski Crystal Bicone Bead

(G): 5052 8mm Fern Green Swarovski Crystal Round Mini Bead

(H): 5053 8mm Fern Green Swarovski Crystal Square Mini Bead

(I): 5051 10 x 8mm Fern Green Swarovski Crystal Oval Mini Bead

(K): 5052 8mm Indicolite Swarovski Crystal Round Mini Bead

(L): 5053 8mm Indicolite Swarovski Crystal Square Mini Bead

(M): 5051 10 x 8mm Indicolite Swarovski Crystal Oval Mini Bead

(N): 5052 8mm Amethyst Swarovski Crystal Round Mini Bead

(O): 5051 10 x 8mm Amethyst Swarovski Crystal Oval Mini Bead

TOOLS

Round-nose pliers

Chain-nose pliers

Wire cutters

TECHNIQUES

Wire-Wrapped Loop (page 122)

Wire-Wrapped Link (page 123)

Opening and Closing a Jump Ring (page 125)

FINISHED LENGTH

7½" (19 cm)

1 Make a wrapped loop on one end of a 3" (7.5 cm) piece of wire and add 1G.

2 Wrap the remaining wire to create a loop on the other side of the bead. Cut off the excess wire to complete your wire-wrapped link.

3 Repeat Steps 1–2 for each Swarovski crystal mini bead for a total of eight wire-wrapped links. Set these links aside.

Add one jump ring to one loop of the fern green mini-bead link.

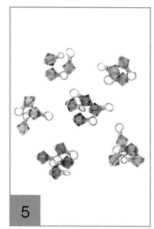

4 Add one Swarovski crystal bicone to a head pin. Make a loop and wrap the wire down to the bead. Cut off the excess wire to complete your wire wrap. This will create one wire-wrapped dangle.

5 Repeat Step 4 for 20 of the remaining bicones.

Note: Leave one 4mm fuchsia bicone to use later in the design.

6 Open a jump ring and add the following items in order: 1M bead link, 1D dangle, 1C dangle, 1G link, and 1A dangle. Close the jump ring.

7 Open another jump ring and add the following items in order: 1N link, 1B dangle, the other side of the M link, 1F dangle, and 1E bicone dangle. Close the jump ring.

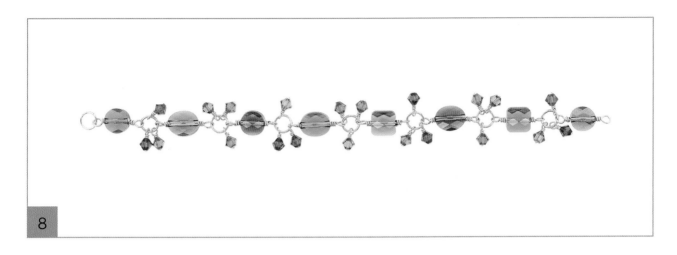

8   Continue adding bicone dangles and mini-bead links as you did in Steps 6 and 7 until all links and dangles have been attached together.

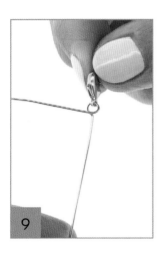  

9   To add the clasp, make a loop on one side of a 3" (7.5 cm) piece of wire. Add the loop of the clasp into the loop of the wire. Wire wrap this loop and cut off the excess wire.

10   Add the remaining fuchsia bicone to the wire. Make a loop and attach the open loop to the indicolite round mini-bead link.

11   Wrap the wire down to the bicone and cut off the excess wire.

Fade INTO You
EARRINGS

Set striking Swarovski rivoli stones in silver bezels to create a pair of pink earrings that fade to perfection.

MATERIALS

2 light rose 12mm crystal rivolis

2 rose 12mm crystal rivolis

2 fuchsia 12mm crystal rivolis

4 rhodium-plated 22.75 x 15.25mm faceted rivoli links

2 rhodium-plated 18.75 x 15.25mm faceted rivoli charms

4 sterling silver 5mm open jump rings 19ga

1 pair sterling silver ear wires with front loop

E6000 adhesive 0.18 oz tube

Shown here:

1122 12mm Light Rose Swarovski Crystal Rivoli Stone

1122 12mm Rose Swarovski Crystal Rivoli Stone

1122 12mm Fuchsia Swarovski Crystal Rivoli Stone

4 Rhodium-Plated 22.75 x 15.25mm Pewter Faceted Rivoli Link by TierraCast®

2 Rhodium-Plated 18.75x15.25mm Pewter Faceted Rivoli Charm by TierraCast®

TOOLS

Chain-nose pliers

TECHNIQUES

Opening and Closing a Jump Ring (page 125)

FINISHED LENGTH

2.75" (7 cm)

1 Add a small drop of glue to one bezel link using a toothpick.

2 Place one light rose rivoli stone in the bezel link.

3 Gently press the rivoli stone so that it is set in the bezel. Let dry completely.

4 Repeat Steps 1–3 for the remaining light rose rivoli stone and the two rose rivoli stones.

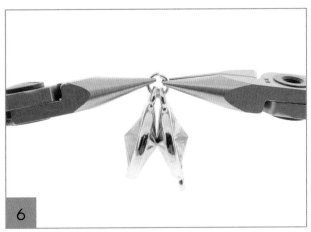

5 Using the two rivoli charms and the fuchsia rivoli stones, repeat Steps 1–3.

6 Build the earring from the bottom up. Use a 5mm jump ring to join one fuchsia charm and one rose link. Close the jump ring.

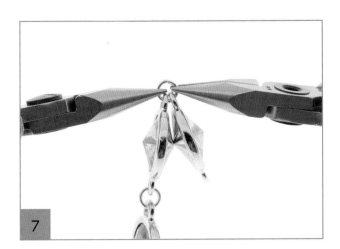

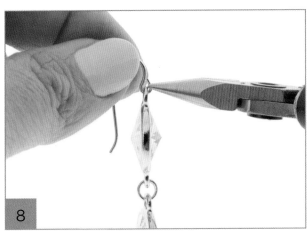

7 Use a 5mm jump ring to join the rose link from Step 6 and one light rose link. Close the jump ring.

8 Attach an ear wire to the light rose link from Step 7. Repeat Steps 6–8 for the second earring.

Emerald Edge
NECKLACE

Designed by Allison Hoffmann

With Swarovski's emerald-cut beads, you can create a necklace fit for a queen but edgy enough to be worn to the club. Emerald green and gunmetal create the perfect blend of elegance and style.

MATERIALS

5 emerald 18 x 12.5mm crystal emerald-cut beads

2 gunmetal-plated 6mm open jump rings 20ga

5 gunmetal-plated 2" (5 cm) eye pins 21ga

1 gunmetal-plated 16 x 12mm toggle clasp

13" (33cm) of gunmetal-plated 5mm double-link cable chains

Shown here:

5515 18 x 12.5mm Emerald Swarovski Crystal Emerald Cut Bead

TOOLS

Round-nose pliers

Chain-nose pliers

Wire cutters

TECHNIQUES

Simple Loop (page 121)

Opening and Closing a Jump Ring (page 125)

FINISHED LENGTH

18" (45.5 cm)

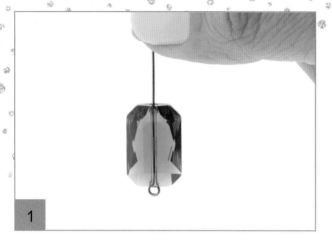

1   Place one emerald-cut bead on an eye pin.

2   Make a simple loop with the remaining wire. Make sure that both loops face the same way. This will create one unit.

3   Repeat Steps 1–2 for a total of five units.

4   Attach each link from Step 3 together by opening and attaching each of the loops created.

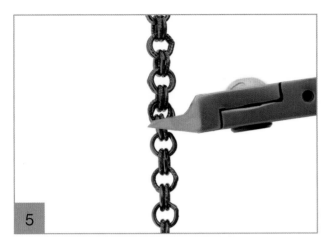 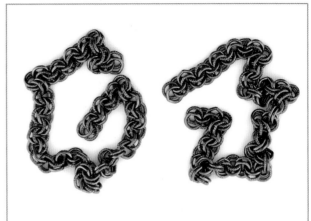

5 Cut two lengths of chain to 6½" (16.5 cm) each.

6 Open the last loop from Step 4 and attach to both loops of one piece of chain. Repeat for the second piece of chain.

7 Open a jump ring and attach the bar end of the toggle clasp and one end of the lengths of chain. Close the jump ring.

8 Open a jump ring and attach the loop end of the toggle clasp and the other length of chain. Close the jump ring.

YOU'RE *Making Me Blush* EARRINGS

Designed by Allison Hoffmann

Three teardrop components covered in soft Swarovski crystals are so sweet, they'll make you blush. These earrings are perfect for a bride-to-be.

MATERIALS

36 blush rose 3mm crystal bicones (A)

36 light silk 3mm crystal bicones (B)

36 vintage rose 3mm bicones (C)

6 gold-filled 20 x 14mm flat teardrop components

4 gold-filled 6mm open jump rings 20.5ga

1 gold-filled 20.5mm french earring hoop with 2mm bead

10′ (3 m) of gold-filled dead-soft wire 28ga

Shown here:

(A): 5328 3mm Blush Rose Swarovski Crystal Bicone Bead

(B): 5328 3mm Light Silk Swarovski Crystal Bicone Bead

(C): 5328 3mm Vintage Rose Swarovski Crystal Bicone Bead

TOOLS

Chain-nose pliers

Wire cutters

TECHNIQUES

Covering a Component (page 124)

Opening and Closing a Jump Ring (page 125)

FINISHED LENGTH

3" (7.5 cm)

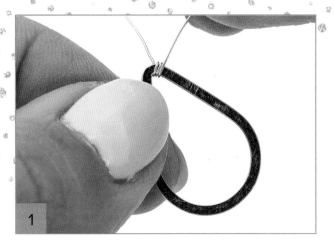

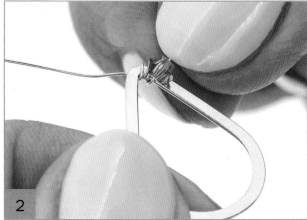

1 Cut a piece of wire 18" (45.5 cm) long. Attach the end of the wire to one teardrop component by wrapping the wire around the component 2–3 times.

2 Add 1A to the wire. Wrap the wire around the component once. Make sure you lay the wire tight next to the bicone.

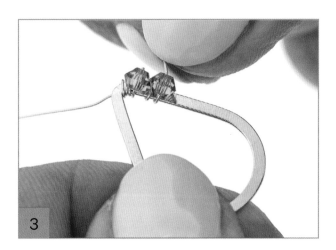

3 Add another A to the wire and wrap the wire around the component once more.

4 Continue adding bicones to the component with a wrap between each bicone. Once all the bicones have been added, finish the wire off by wrapping it around the component 2–3 times. Cut off the excess wire.

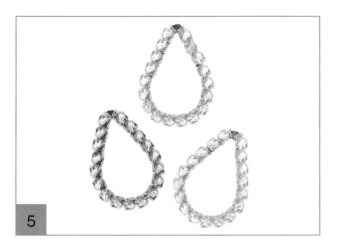

5 Repeat Steps 1–4 for the remaining two components. Each component should have one color of bicone beads on them.

6 Begin attaching the covered components together by opening a jump ring. Add the tip of the blush rose-covered teardrop component and the base of the vintage rose-covered teardrop component to the jump ring. Close the jump ring.

7 Open a jump ring. Add the tip of the vintage rose-covered teardrop component from Step 6 and the base of the light silk covered teardrop component to the jump ring. Close the jump ring.

8 Attach an ear wire to the tip of the light silk-covered teardrop component from Step 7.

Repeat Steps 1–8 for the second earring.

Midnight IN Paradise

EARRINGS

Designed by Cody Westfall

A figure eight of beautiful crystal beads strung onto beading wire will make a big statement while still being lightweight and easy to wear. Switch up the colors and make several pairs of these earrings to go with every outfit.

MATERIALS

24 crystal paradise shine 3mm crystal rounds (A)

28 crystal paradise shine 4mm crystal rounds (B)

12 crystal paradise shine 6mm crystal rounds (C)

2 crystal paradise shine 8mm crystal rounds (D)

2 crystal paradise shine 10mm crystal rounds (E)

1 pair sterling silver 21mm french hoops with 2mm bead

2 sterling silver 2 x 2mm crimp-beads

2 sterling silver 3.5mm crimp bead covers

12" (30.5 cm) of clear beading wire .014" dia.

Shown here:

(A): 5000 3mm Crystal Paradise Shine Swarovski Crystal Round Bead

(B): 5000 4mm Crystal Paradise Shine Swarovski Crystal Round Bead

(C): 5000 6mm Crystal Paradise Shine Swarovski Crystal Round Bead

(D): 5000 8mm Crystal Paradise Shine Swarovski Crystal Round Bead

(E): 5000 10mm Crystal Paradise Shine Swarovski Crystal Round Bead

TOOLS

Crimping pliers

Wire cutters

TECHNIQUES

Crimping (page 120)

Using a Crimp Cover (page 121)

FINISHED LENGTH

2½" (6.5 cm)

 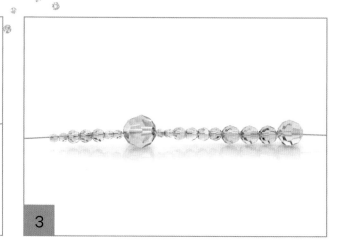

1 Cut 6" (15 cm) of beading wire.

String these beads in the following sequence onto the beading wire: 2A, 3B, 2A.

2 String 1E.

3 String these beads in the following sequence onto the beading wire: 2A, 4B, 3C, 1D.

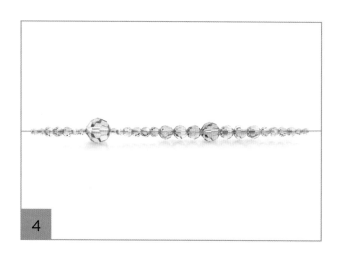 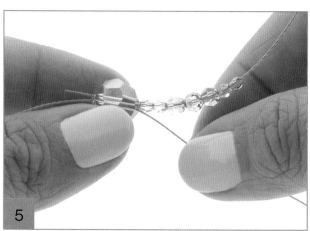

4 String these beads in the following sequence onto the beading wire: 3C, 4B, 2A.

5 String the beading wire through the E in Step 2 in the opposite direction.

6   String these beads in the following sequence onto the beading wire: 2A, 3B, 2A.

7   Add a crimp bead to the wire. Pass both ends of the beading wire through the crimp bead in opposite directions. Use your crimping tool to crimp the bead.

8   Cut off the excess beading wire.

9   Cover the crimp bead with a crimp cover.

10   Attach an ear wire near the crimp cover. Repeat Steps 1–10 for the second earring.

Endless Possibilities
NECKLACE

Designed by Samantha Slater

Combine three different crystal pendants in a multistrand necklace. The various lengths of chain make this necklace so versatile and easy to wear with almost any neckline.

MATERIALS

1 crystal paradise shine 12mm crystal circle pendant

1 peridot 16mm crystal pear-shaped pendant

1 crystal vitrail light 30mm crystalactite pendant

1 silver-plated 9.5 x 5.5mm lobster-claw clasp

58" (147.5 cm) of imitation rhodium–plated 2mm oval cable chain

2 silver-plated 4mm open jump rings 21ga

1 silver-plated 5mm open jump ring 21ga

2 silver-plated 7mm open jump rings 19ga

Shown here:

6428 12mm Crystal Paradise Shine Swarovski Crystal Xilion Circle Pendant

6106 16mm Peridot Swarovski Crystal Pear-Shaped Pendant

6017/G 30mm Crystal Vitrail Light Swarovski Crystal Crystalactite Pendant

TOOLS

Chain-nose pliers

Wire cutters

TECHNIQUES

Opening and Closing a Jump Ring (page 125)

FINISHED LENGTH

17½" (44.5 cm)

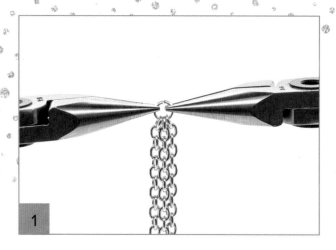

1 Cut 3 lengths of chain to the following lengths:

17" (43 cm)

18¾" (47.5 cm)

22" (56 cm)

Open one 4mm jump ring. Add the ends of the three lengths of chain. Close the jump ring.

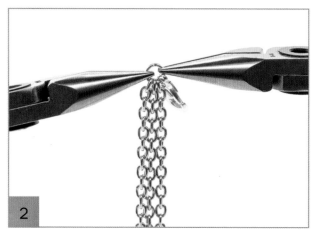

2 Open one 4mm jump ring. Add the other ends of the three lengths of chain and the clasp. Close the jump ring.

3 Open one 7mm jump ring. Attach the crystal crystalactite pendant and attach it to the longest length of chain from Step 2. Close the jump ring.

4 Repeat Step 3 to add the other two pendants with the two 5mm jump rings to the remaining two lengths of chain.

Hanging
BY A Thread
EARRINGS

Simplicity and style meet in this earring design. A single crystal bead hangs from an ear string. The chain hangs delicately behind the ear for an added element.

MATERIALS

2 amethyst 14 x 9.5mm crystal emerald-cut beads

2 silver-plated 2" (5 cm) head pins with 2mm ball

1 pair sterling silver 3" (7.5 cm) U-top box chain ear string with ring

Shown here:

5515 14 x 9.5mm Amethyst Swarovski Crystal Emerald Cut Bead

TOOLS

Round-nose pliers

Chain-nose pliers

Wire cutters

TECHNIQUES

Wire-Wrapped Loop (page 122)

FINISHED LENGTH

$2\frac{1}{2}$" (6.5 cm)

1 Place 1 amethyst crystal emerald-cut bead on a head pin.

2 Begin making a wire-wrapped loop with the wire. Make the loop but do not wrap the wire.

TIP

If the hole in your bead is too big and the head of the head pin slips through the hole, try adding a small spacer bead then add the larger bead.

3 Attach the ring on the ear string to the loop created in Step 2.

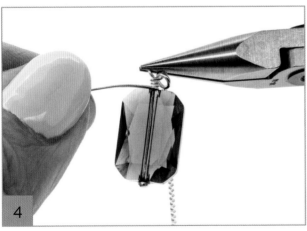

4 Wrap the wire to complete the wire-wrapped loop. Cut off the excess wire.

Repeat Steps 1-4 for the second earring.

Glamorous
EARRINGS

Delicate chain fringe drapes from a rich green crystal pavé bead. The on-trend design will add playful movement to your party outfit.

MATERIALS

2 dark moss green 10mm crystal pavé beads

30" (76 cm) of gold-plated brass 1.5mm twisted helix chain

1 pair gold-filled 16mm leverback earrings with shells

6" (15 cm) of gold-filled half-hard wire 24ga

Shown here:

10mm Dark Moss Green Swarovski Crystal Pavé Bead

TOOLS

Round-nose pliers

Chain-nose pliers

Wire cutters

TECHNIQUES

Wire-Wrapped Link (page 123)

FINISHED LENGTH

2¾" (7 cm)

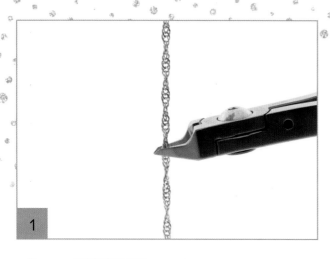

1 Cut a 1½" (3.8 cm) length of chain.

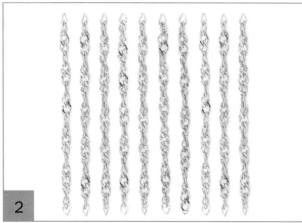

2 Repeat Step 1 for a total of ten lengths of chain.

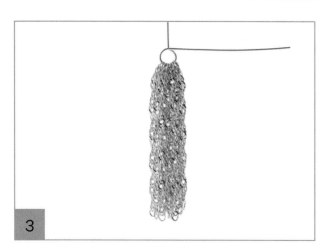

3 Use a 3" (7.5 cm) piece of wire and begin making a large wire loop. Do not wrap the loop. Add all ten lengths of chain into the loop created.

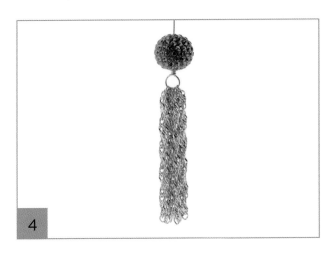

4   Wrap the loop created in Step 3. Place one crystal pavé bead on the wire.

5   Finish the wire-wrapped link by making a loop on top of the bead, wrapping the wire and cutting off the excess wire.

6   Attach an ear wire to the loop created in Step 5.

Repeat Steps 1–6 for the second earring.

Flair FOR Florals
NECKLACE

Designed by Samantha Slater

Whether you're going to a Spring wedding or a tea party, this charming floral necklace will be the center of attention. Show off your feminine flair for beautiful blossoms.

MATERIALS

2 rose AB 3mm crystal bicones

2 rose opal 2.5 x 6.5mm flower spacer pressed-glass beads

3 Indian pink 3mm crystal bicones

3 fuchsia 2.5 x 6.5mm flower spacer pressed-glass beads

3 fuchsia 4mm crystal bicones

3 ruby peacock 6 x 9mm day lily pressed-glass beads

4 fuchsia AB2X 4mm crystal bicones

4 rose/fuchsia lumine 8 x 12mm day lily pressed glass beads

2 fuchsia 6mm crystal bicones

2 rose 6mm crystal bicones

17 sterling silver 2" (5 cm) head pins 22ga

2 sterling silver 4mm open jump rings 22ga

19½" (49.5 cm) of sterling silver 2mm cable chain

1 sterling silver 10mm round toggle clasp

Shown here:

5328 3mm Rose AB Swarovski Crystal Bicone Bead

2.5 x 6.5mm Rose Opal Flower Spacer Czech Pressed-Glass Bead

5328 3mm Indian Pink Swarovski Crystal Bicone Bead

2.5 x 6.5mm Fuchsia Flower Spacer Czech Pressed-Glass Bead

5328 4mm Fuchsia Swarovski Crystal Bicone Bead

6 x 9mm Ruby Peacock Day Lily Czech Pressed-Glass Bead

5328 4mm Fuchsia AB2X Swarovski Crystal Bicone Bead

8 x 12mm Rose/Fuchsia Lumine Day Lily Czech Pressed-Glass Bead

5328 6mm Fuchsia Swarovski Crystal Bicone Bead

5328 6mm Rose Swarovski Crystal Bicone Bead

TOOLS

Round-nose pliers

Chain-nose pliers

Wire cutters

TECHNIQUES

Simple Loop (page 121)

Opening and Closing a Jump Ring (page 125)

FINISHED LENGTH

20" (51 cm)

1 Place one 4mm fuchsia AB2x crystal bicone and one 8 x 12mm rose/fuchsia lumine day lily glass bead on a head pin.

2 Create a simple loop with the remaining wire. This is one large flower dangle unit.

Tip: Make sure the loop is large enough to slip over the chain.

3 Repeat Steps 1–2 to create the remaining units. You will have a total of 17 units:

3 units–3mm Indian pink crystal bicone and 2.5 x 6.5mm fuchsia flower glass bead (A)

2 units–3mm rose AB crystal bicone and 2.5 x 6.5mm rose opal flower glass bead (B)

4 units–4mm fuchsia crystal bicone and 6 x 9mm ruby peacock flower glass bead (C)

4 units–4mm fuchsia AB2X crystal bicone and 8 x 12mm rose/fuchsia lumine day lily glass bead (D)

2 units–6mm fuchsia crystal bicone bead (E)

2 units–6mm rose crystal bicone bead (F)

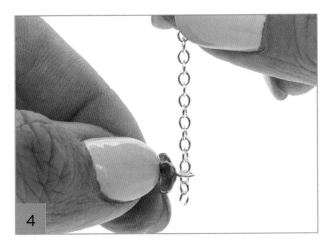

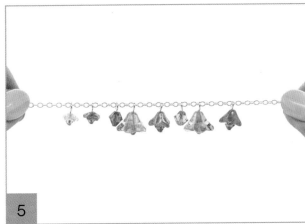

4 Using a 19½" (49.5 cm) piece of chain, begin adding the units created in Step 3.

5 Add the units in the following order: B, A, E, D, C, F, D, C.

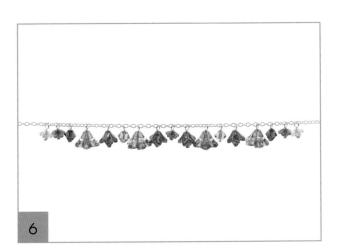

6 Add one A unit.

Add the units in the following order: C, D, F, C, D, E, A, B.

7 Finish the necklace by opening a jump ring and adding it to one end of the chain. Attach the bar side of the toggle clasp. Close the jump ring.

8 Open another jump ring and add it to the other end of the chain. Attach the loop side of the toggle clasp. Close the jump ring.

Denim Ice
NECKLACE

Designed by Allison Hoffmann

You will be cool as ice wearing this multi-strand necklace dripping with icy blue Swarovski crystals and rhinestone chain.

MATERIALS

16 denim blue 6mm crystal rounds (A)

16 crystal blue shade 6mm crystal rounds (B)

16 denim blue 8mm crystal rounds (C)

14 crystal blue shade 8mm crystal rounds (D)

62 silver-plated 2" (5 cm) head pins 21ga

2 silver-plated 5mm open jump rings 18ga

2 silver-plated 10mm open jump rings 18ga

1 silver-plated 16 x 12mm toggle clasp

16½" (42 cm) of silver-plated 3.5mm crystal AB bezel rhinestone chain

18¾" (47 cm) rhodium-plated 3.5mm oval cable chain

10" (25.5 cm) rhodium-plated 5mm oval cable chain

4 silver-plated 7.5 x 3mm spring-ring chain end for crystal rhinestone chain

Shown here:

(A): 5000 6mm Denim Blue Swarovski Crystal Round Bead

(B): 5000 6mm Crystal Blue Shade Swarovski Crystal Round Bead

(C): 5000 8mm Denim Blue Swarovski Crystal Round Bead

(D): 5000 8mm Crystal Blue Shade Swarovski Crystal Round Bead

TOOLS

Round-nose pliers

Chain-nose pliers

Wire cutters

TECHNIQUES

Simple Loop (page 121)

Opening and Closing a Jump Ring (page 125)

FINISHED LENGTH

19" (48.5 cm)

1

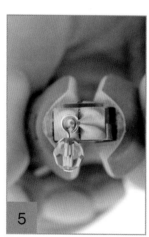

2

3

1 Cut one 7" (18 cm) and one 9½" (24 cm) length of the crystal rhinestone chain. Lay one end of a chain in the spring-ring chain end.

2 Fold the tabs of the spring ring chain end around the rhinestone chain to secure it.

3 Attach a 5mm jump ring to the spring-ring chain end.

Repeat for all four ends of the rhinestone chain. Set aside.

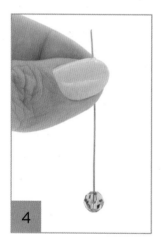

4

5

6

7

4 Place an A onto a head pin.

5 Make a simple loop with the remaining wire. This will make one round dangle.

6 Repeat Steps 4–5 for all of the crystal beads. You will have a total of 16 A dangles, 16 B dangles, 16 C dangles, and 14 D dangles.

7 Cut an 8" (20.5 cm) piece of the rhodium-plated 3.5mm oval cable chain. Add one C dangle to the center link of the chain.

8

9

8 Continue adding dangles to every other link of the chain, working from the center out. Add the beads in the following order on each side of the center dangle:

1 D dangle	1 D dangle	1 D dangle
1 A dangle	1 A dangle	1 A dangle
1 B dangle	1 B dangle	1 B dangle
1 C dangle	1 C dangle	

Set aside.

9 Cut an 11" (28 cm) piece of the rhodium-plated 3.5mm oval cable chain. Add 1 C dangle to the center link of the chain. Add dangles to every other link of the chain, working from the center out. Add the beads in the following order on each side of the center dangle:

1 D dangle	1 C dangle	1 B dangle
1 A dangle	1 D dangle	1 C dangle
1 B dangle	1 A dangle	1 D dangle
1 C dangle	1 B dangle	1 A dangle
1 D dangle	1 C dangle	1 B dangle
1 A dangle	1 D dangle	
1 B dangle	1 A dangle	

Set aside.

10 Cut two 5" (12.5 cm) pieces of the rhodium-plated 5mm oval cable chain. Set aside.

11 Open one 10mm jump ring. Add one end of the longer beaded chain from Step 9, one end of the longer rhinestone chain from Step 3, one end of the shorter beaded chain from Step 8, one end of the shorter rhinestone chain from Step 3, and one length of chain from Step 10. Close the jump ring.

12 Repeat Step 11 with the other 10mm jump ring and the remaining ends of chain.

13 Attach each end of the toggle clasp to the chain using a 5mm jump ring.

GLOSSARY

BEADS

Crystal

Crystal beads are made of a synthetic, glass-like product created by combining and processing a variety of minerals. After the crystal is created, state-of-the-art techniques are used to cut the crystal and form impeccable facets, giving it its incredible sparkle and reflective qualities.

Czech Pressed-Glass Beads

Czech pressed-glass beads are made in the Czech Republic by pressing molten glass into molds. These molds come in various shapes such as round, oval, teardrop, flower, and leaf.

Fire Polished Glass Beads

Fire-polished glass beads are Czech pressed-glass beads that have multiple facets. The facets catch the light to add sparkle to your project. These are a great alternative to crystal beads.

Freshwater Pearls

Freshwater pearls have been grown in pearl mussels that naturally live in freshwater. Pearls come in many shapes and sizes—rice, round, potato, button, and stick are just a few. In nature, pearls come in a range of colors from white, cream, and pale pink to natural tints of yellow, green, blue, and black. Using an electroplating process, freshwater pearls can be treated to create gorgeous fashion colors—fuchsia, purple, blue, yellow, and green. Unlike dyeing, electroplating results in a permanent color on the pearl.

Gemstone (Semiprecious Stones)

Semiprecious" refers to gemstones that occur naturally in the earth but are not considered precious. All gemstone beads have been treated in some way, usually with heat to enhance the stone's natural color and harden it. Gemstones are more plentiful than precious stones and are therefore less expensive. Some examples of popular gemstones are amethyst, peridot, aquamarine, carnelian, and garnet.

Metal Beads

Metal beads are great to use in your piece of jewelry. They come in various sizes, shapes, and metals, making them useable as focal beads or accent beads. Metal beads include beads made of materials such as sterling silver, gold-filled, silver-filled, pewter, brass, and base metal, to name a few.

FINDINGS

Crimp-Bead

Crimp-beads are small tubular or round beads that are used to secure a clasp to flexible beading wire or other stringing material that cannot be knotted. When crimped with a crimping tool, a crimp bead will have smooth, rounded edges and will be most securely attached.

Crimp Bead Cover

Crimp bead covers conceal crimp beads, adding a polished, professional touch to your jewelry. Use pliers to gently squeeze the two sides of a cover together over a crimp bead.

Eye Pin

Eye pins are similar to head pins except the wire ends with a small loop instead of a head. The loop can be attached to another eye pin, head pin, clasp, or other finding. Links can then be connected to form chains or long dangles. Eye pins come in different gauges (usually 20–26 gauge) and lengths.

Head Pin

Head pins are straight pieces of wire with a flat, round, or decorative end. Slide one or more beads onto a head pin and form a wrapped or simple loop on the open end. The head keeps the beads from sliding off. You can connect these dangles to other findings or chain to create earrings, necklaces, or bracelets. Head pins come in different gauges (usually 20–26 gauge) and lengths.

Jump Ring

Jump rings are small rings of wire used to attach components or charms to other elements. They can also be used as a catch for clasps such as lobster-claw and S clasps. Open jump rings can be opened and reclosed with pliers. Closed jump rings are stronger because they have been soldered, forming a continuous circle.

Lobster-Claw Clasp

Lobster-claw clasps are among the most popular clasp choices. Available in many sizes, styles, and materials, lobster-claw clasps use tension from a spring-loaded mechanism to keep the clasp securely closed. The claw catches a jump ring, loop, or piece of chain on the other end of a bracelet or necklace.

Multistrand Clasp

These clasps work the same way as single-strand clasps except that they have multiple loops available to attach to more than one strand of wire or thread.

Toggle Clasp

Toggle clasps are an easy-to-fasten, popular, secure way to finish a necklace or bracelet. Attach the toggle bar to one end of your jewelry and the toggle ring to the other. To fasten, simply pivot the bar so that it can slip inside the ring, then pivot the bar again to secure it. The bar is longer than the diameter of the ring to keep the clasp secured.

WIRE

Beading Wire

Beading wire is one of the best, most commonly used stringing materials. It is created by coating multiple strands of very fine steel cable wire with nylon. The result is a strong but supple stringing material. Since it is a steel-cable wire, you will not be able to finish it with a knot. Instead, you will need to use a crimp bead or crimp tube and crimping pliers. Also, since it is coated in nylon, there are various colors available. The most popular color is clear so that you see the color of the steel-cable wire underneath. But beading wire comes in a rainbow of colors.

Gauge

Gauge is the most common measurement of wire thickness used in the United States. The smaller the gauge, the thicker the wire. For example, 16-gauge wire is thicker than 22-gauge.

Memory Wire

Memory wire is a hardened-steel wire that retains its shape no matter how many times it is flexed. This is a fun, easy wire to use for your projects. Start your memory wire by putting a small loop on one end. The loop will help prevent beads from falling off. Then all you have to do is add beads to the wire. Finish the wire the same way as you began, with a simple loop. Be aware that since memory wire is hardened steel, you will need to use special memory-wire cutters. If you use any other wire cutters, the memory wire will mar the cutters and make them unusable.

TOOLS

Chain-Nose Pliers

Chain-nose pliers are a necessary staple in any beader's toolbox. These useful pliers have flat jaws that taper to a point and are used to grip and bend wire. Unlike the pliers you may be borrowing from the family toolbox, jewelry pliers have a smooth finish that won't mar your wire.

Crimping Pliers

Crimping pliers are used specifically for securing crimp beads to the ends of flexible beading wire. Crimping pliers, used with tubular crimp beads, create smooth, rounded crimps.

Memory-Wire Cutters

Memory-wire cutters are a hard-wire shear perfect for memory wire and other hard wires. Because of its shear-type action, this cutter will not nick or dull like ordinary cutters when used on hard wire.

Round-Nose Pliers

Round-nose pliers have tapered, conical jaws for making round wire loops. Use these pliers to create beaded drops and charms. They are an essential tool for any wire-working techniques such as creating simple loops or wire wrapping.

Wire Cutters

Wire cutters have sharp blades that will snip wire with a clean, close cut that leaves no burrs that can snag or scratch.

TECHNIQUES

CRIMPING

Crimping is the fastest, most secure way to create a beaded necklace or bracelet. Use crimp beads or crimp tubes to secure a clasp to the end of beading wire. Using beading wire and a crimp bead will give you a finished piece that is both strong and professional-looking.

1 String a crimp bead onto the beading wire.

2 String one end of the clasp onto the beading wire. Then go back through the crimp bead, creating a loop around the clasp.

3 Make sure that the wires are lying parallel to each other. Place the crimp bead into the back notch of the pliers. Squeeze the pliers so that the crimp bead closes around the pieces of wire.

4 Turn the bead a quarter turn and place the crimp bead in the front notch. Gently squeeze the pliers so that it squishes the crimp bead. This will fold the crimped bead over on itself.

5 Use the wire cutter to trim the small tail of the beading wire even with the crimp bead. Now, you can start or finish creating your piece of jewelry.

USING A CRIMP COVER

A crimp cover is not necessary. However, it will give your jewelry that extra expert touch. The crimp cover is used to go around the crimp bead to hide or disguise the crimp bead as a small, round bead.

1 Place the crimp-bead cover in the front notch of the crimping pliers with the opening facing out. Place the crimped bead inside the crimp-bead cover.

2 Gently squeeze the pliers just until the crimp-bead cover is completely closed.

SIMPLE LOOP

A simple loop is used to create a dangle or link with a bead. A loop can be created with wire, a head pin, or an eye pin. I recommend using wire that is 22-gauge or thicker.

1 Place a bead or beads onto a head pin. Cut the head pin, leaving ³⁄₈".

2 Bend the wire at the top of the bead to a 90° angle with chain-nose pliers or your fingers.

3 Grasp the end of the wire with round-nose pliers so the wire is flush with the tool.

4 Rotate the pliers to form a loop. Continue turning the wire until a complete loop is formed.

> **TIP:**
>
> *To make a smaller loop, work closer to the tip of the round-nose pliers. If you want to make a larger loop, start with a piece of wire longer than ³⁄₈" and make the loop further back from the tip of the round-nose pliers.*

WIRE-WRAPPED LOOP

A wire-wrapped loop is a secure way of creating a dangle or link with a bead. Create a loop and then wrap the wire to completely close the loop.

1 Place a bead or beads on the head pin. Remember to have at least an inch of wire above the last bead. Using the tips of your chain-nose pliers, grab the wire directly above the beads.

2 With your finger, push the wire to a 90° angle.

3 Using your round-nose pliers, grasp the wire right at the bend.

4 Pull the wire around the round-nose pliers until it is almost pointing directly down. Reposition your pliers by opening your round-nose pliers (but do not pull the pliers out of the loop) and pivot your pliers so the bottom tip is on the top. Continue pulling the wire around the nose of the pliers until the loop is completely round.

5 To then wrap the loop, grip the loop with the chain-nose pliers and grip the wire with your fingers.

6 Wrap the wire around the head pin. Continue wrapping the wire down to the bead.

7 Using the wire cutters, cut off the extra wire as close as you can to the beads.

WIRE-WRAPPED LINK

Using a wire-wrapped link to connect beads together is a very secure and attractive connection. By wrapping the loop, the link or clasp connected into the loop will not slide out. Use the link to create earrings, necklaces, and bracelets.

1 Cut a 3–4" piece of wire. Grasp your wire about 1½" down from the top with your chain-nose pliers. With your finger, push the wire to a 90° angle.

2 Using your round-nose pliers, grasp the wire right at the bend. Pull the wire around the round-nose pliers until it is almost pointing directly down.

3 Reposition your pliers by opening your round-nose pliers (but do not pull the pliers out of the loop) and pivot your pliers so the bottom tip is on the top. Continue pulling the wire around the nose of the pliers until the loop is completely round.

4 Attach a link, chain or clasp into the loop.

5 To then wrap the loop, grip the loop with the chain-nose pliers and grip the wire with your fingers. Wrap the short wire around the long wire about three wraps.

6 Using the wire cutters, cut off the extra wire as close as you can.

7 Slide a bead or beads on the wire. Using the tips of your chain-nose pliers, grab the wire directly above the beads. With your finger, push the wire to a 90° angle.

8 Using your round-nose pliers, grasp the wire right at the bend. Create a loop with the remaining wire.

(continued on next page)

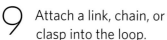

9 Attach a link, chain, or clasp into the loop.

10 To then wrap the loop, grip the loop with the chain-nose pliers and grip the wire with your fingers. Wrap the wire around the base wire. Continue wrapping the wire down to the bead.

Using the wire cutters, cut off the extra wire as close as you can to the beads.

COVERING A COMPONENT

Use wire to add beads to a component. This is a great way to add an element of color and texture to a metal component. These components can be used in earrings, necklaces or bracelets. Simply use a thin-gauge, soft wire to attach the beads securely to the component.

1 Use a 26- or 28-gauge, dead-soft piece of wire. Cut the wire to length depending on the size of the component. To begin, anchor the wire to the component with two wraps.

2 String a bead onto the wire. Rest the bead on the surface of the component. Bring the wire over the top of the component.

3 Bring the wire behind the component and pull it up through the middle of the component. Make one complete wrap around the component with the wire.

4 Bring the wire up through the middle of the component. String another bead onto the wire.

5 Continue wrapping the wire and adding beads around the component.

To finish, anchor the end of the wire by making two wire wraps. Once the wire is anchored, cut the end of the wire with the wire cutters.

You may want to add a small drop of jewelry glue to the cut end of the wire. This will help prevent the wire from snagging and coming apart.

OPENING AND CLOSING A JUMP RING

To open a jump ring, grasp each side of its opening with a pair of pliers. Don't pull apart. Instead, twist in opposite directions so that you can open and close it without distorting the ring's shape.

CONTRIBUTORS

ALLISON HOFFMANN is a mother, artist, and jewelry designer who resides in Seattle, Washington. Her passion has been painting and designing jewelry as a creative outlet for well over a decade. She sells her art and jewelry around the Seattle area and has been published in several magazines such as *Jewelry Stringing and BeadStyle*.

CODY WESTFALL dabbled in many different beading techniques before finding her calling in wire-wrapping, riveting, and dapping designs. Her jewelry has been featured in both domestic and international beading magazines. Cody currently lives in Seattle's Queen Anne neighborhood and teaches metalworking classes at the Fusion Beads retail store.

KATIE WALI has been creating with beads for over twenty years. She loves to bead with bright, bold colors, and her favorite techniques are right-angle weave, wire wrapping and bead crochet. She enjoys the endless possibilities and creativity beading brings to her. You can find her designs featured in a number of publications.

SAMANTHA SLATER Along with continually challenging herself through art, music, books, and general creative endeavors, it was a move to Seattle, Washington, from South Africa that drew Samantha to jewelry making. She finally found a medium in which she can express her yearning for beauty, her love of art, and her desire for perfection all in one.

SOURCES FOR SUPPLIES

Check your favorite bead retailer.
Visit your local bead store or jewelry supply store or check out the following resources.

Fusion Beads,Inc.
fusionbeads.com

Fusion Beads is an online beading and jewelry-supply store specializing in Swarovski crystals, seed beads, gemstones, pearls, glass beads, components, tools, and so much more! Offering projects and techniques for all skill levels and beading interests.

Swarovski Crystal
www.create-your-style.com

Swarovski is the premium brand for the finest crystal embellishments since 1895. Recognized for its innovative excellence and its collaborations with top-class designers and brands in fashion, jewelry, and accessories. Born out of a passion for detail and high-precision cutting, these precious crystals impart refined glamour to everything they embellish.

TierraCast®,Inc.
www.tierracast.com

TierraCast is a wholesale-only manufacturer of components jewelry makers love to use. Located in Northern California since 1978, the company is dedicated to quality product, and sharing techniques and information with beaders worldwide.

INDEX

Nunn Design

www.nunndesign.com

Nunn Design is an innovative wholesale jewelry-findings company committed to providing quality products that can be used with a variety of jewelry-making mediums. All of Nunn Design's cast findings are made in the United States. Be inspired with free tutorials, videos, newsletters, and a fully gallery of jewelry samples that inspires and nurtures your creativity.

METRIC CONVERSION CHART

To convert:	to:	multiply by:
Inches	Centimeters	2.54
Centimeters	Inches	0.4
Feet	Centimeters	30.5
Centimeters	Feet	0.03
Yards	Meters	0.9
Meters	Yards	1.1

a content + ecommerce company

www.fwcommunity.com

20 19 18 17 16 5 4 3 2 1

Distributed in Canada by Fraser Direct
100 Armstrong Avenue
Georgetown, ON, Canada L7G 5S4
Tel: (905) 877-4411

Distributed in the U.K. and Europe by F&W MEDIA INTERNATIONAL
Brunel House, Newton Abbot, Devon, TQ12 4PU, England
Tel: (+44) 1626 323200, Fax: (+44) 1626 323319
E-mail: enquiries@fwmedia.com

SRN: 16JM06
ISBN-13: 978-1-63250-421-0

Editorial Director: Kerry Bogert
Acquisitions Editor: Amelia Johanson
Editor: Erica Smith
Art Director: Elisabeth Lariviere
Cover Designer: Sylvia McArdle
Interior Designer: Sylvia McArdle
Photographers: Joysha Fajardo and Devin Stein
Project and Process Stylist: Lindsay Burke
Technical Editor and Illustrator: Bonnie Brooks

JEWELRY FOR ANY OCCASION!

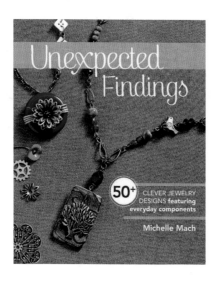

50+ Clever Jewelry Designs featuring everyday components

Michelle Mach

ISBN: 978-1-62033-600-7
Price: $22.99

50 Designs Using Leather, Ribbon, and Cords

Erin Siegel

ISBN: 978-1-59668-498-0
Price: $22.99

***Jewelry Stringing* Magazine** is published quarterly. Each issue of includes more than 70 beautifully strung accessories, accompanied by clear step-by-step instructions and spreads that give beaders ideas and inspiration. The projects range from quick but intriguing necklaces, bracelets, and earrings that can be accomplished in an hour to more complex patterns that may take an entire weekend to complete.

Beading Daily is a vibrant, online beading community offering free beading projects, tutorials, expert advice, and the latest bead/jewelry trends.